Practical Information

Comprehension and Composition Practice

B J Thomas

Edward Arnold

First published 1977 by
Edward Arnold (Publishers) Ltd
41 Bedford Square, London WC1 3DQ

Reprinted 1978, 1979 (twice)

Set IBM 10pt Century by Tek-Art, Croydon,
Surrey.
Printed in Great Britain by Unwin Brothers
Ltd, Old Woking, Surrey.

Acknowledgments
The publishers would like to thank the follow-
ing for permission to reproduce copyright
material (unit number in brackets): (1) British
Rail, Eastern Region; (2) London Transport;
(3, 18) extract from 'Britain: A Traveller's
Guide' published by the British Tourist
Authority; (4) British Rail Hovercraft Ltd;
(5, 6, 7) Post Office; (9, 14) taken from 'How
to Live in Britain' by permission of the British
Council; (10) The Royal Society for the
Prevention of Accidents and HMSO; (11)
Brighton Overseas Students Centre; (12) ILEA;
(13, 30) taken from 'Studying in Britain' by
permission of the British Council; (15, 16) The
Health Education Council; (17) reproduced
from the Highway Code by permission of the
Controller of Her Majesty's Stationery Office;
(19) Godfrey Davis; (20) National Westminster
Bank Ltd; (21) Barclays Bank Ltd;
(22) Wellington Museum; (23) Westminster
City Libraries; (24) from 'A Guide for Visitors
to the Galleries' published by HMSO and
reproduced by permission of the Rt Hon the
Speaker; (25) Oxford City Council; (27, 29)
HMSO; (28) Dept of Health and Social
Security.

British Library Cataloguing in Publication Data

Thomas, B J
    Practical information: comprehension and
    composition practice.
    ISBN 0-7131-0151-2
    1. Title
    428'.2'4   PE1128
    English language - Composition and exercises
    English language - Text-books for foreigners

Contents

Approximate indication of level of difficulty: E Easy   M Medium   A Advanced

Teacher's notes

Purpose

The purpose of this book is to give overseas students the opportunity to practise with current informational English of a type they will need to understand if they are going to:

a visit Britain or are in Britain already;
b take examinations such as Cambridge First Certificate or Proficiency;
c work in jobs needing a knowledge of English.

It also gives a very practical introduction to many basic aspects of modern British life. The book is designed for students of Intermediate to Advanced level, that is from a level before Cambridge First Certificate to a level after it.

Grading

The thirty units contain a variety of different topics presented in different ways. The exercise sections are not standardized or uniformly graded, though the units tend to get more difficult through the book. A note next to each item in the list of contents gives an approximate indication of difficulty. Teachers should look carefully at units before any classwork to see how difficult the text is and what kind of exercises follow.

Exercises

In most units, immediately after each text are COMPREHENSION exercises which require the student to read and understand the text. Following these are oral and written COMPOSITION exercises for use, at the teacher's discretion, to give active reinforcement practice.

Every topic is briefly introduced at the beginning of the exercise section. Teachers are strongly advised to use this and their own knowledge to interest the students in the topic before any reading or exercise work is done.

Comprehension section

This consists mainly of open-ended, 'true or false' and vocabulary/register exercises. It is expected that students will attempt all exercises in this section. Only by doing so and achieving a thorough understanding of the text will they be prepared for the exercises in the composition section.

Open-ended questions
These can be treated in a number of different ways. The students can be required individually, in pairs or groups to find the answers. Answers may be given orally, orally from brief notes or in full-sentence form. This can be done as homework, classwork or a combination of the two. It is up to the teacher to choose the method which best suits the class and the text. It might be beneficial to vary the treatment.

However the teacher is advised that this exercise is one of comprehension and corresponds to a normal, everyday activity. The teacher who asks for full-sentence answers must be aware that, though this may be a valid exercise, it extends the exercise beyond its original aim of comprehension.

In giving their answers students should be encouraged not simply to use phrases taken directly from the text but to use normal conversational English. Many questions are answered most naturally with a single word or short phrase.

'True or false' exercises
These correspond much less to any natural comprehension process and are included to add variety and to give some opportunity for students to work with examination-type exercises.

Vocabulary/register exercises
Register is important throughout this book. These exercises, in which students have to explain words and phrases from the text, are important and useful provided that students realize that they are exercises in register. Students are being given words and phrases which were originally included in the text because of their appropriateness to the

required (usually formal) style. The student should not explain them with words of the same register but in the language of ordinary conversation.

Students should also be discouraged from 'explaining' a phrase by mechanically replacing each word in it with another. For example, 'on a partnership basis', is not explained by 'on a foundation of sharing'. 'Those seeking entry' is not made clearer by 'those looking for entry'. And neither attempt would do anything for a student's English. 'Each person playing an equal part' and 'people trying to get in' do explain, and would demonstrate a student's true appreciation of the basic meanings.

These questions are difficult. First efforts should be guided by the teacher. But with the teacher's help students can profit in their awareness of the language and in their own use of it.

Composition section

In these exercises students actively use what they have learnt in the comprehension section. At the same time they practise important skills such as giving talks and writing letters, summaries and compositions. The emphasis is on giving explanations.

Exercises marked (O) are to be done orally. Those marked (O/W) are primarily for oral use but can also be done in writing, possibly orally first as preparation for written answers. Those marked (W) are for written work.

Teachers may well decide to choose one oral followed by one or two written exercises from this section but should keep in mind the possibility of giving an additional exercise at some interval after the unit has been dealt with so that students are not permitted to forget what they have learnt from the unit.

Oral exercises
These, marked (O), ask students to explain a part or all of the topic in the text. In some early units (1, 2, 4, 8, 11) this entails expansion. More often it requires a form of oral summary.

Students should be encouraged to make quick, brief notes from which to talk. This will prevent them from depending on the original written form. Also note-making is an

excellent exercise in itself for general comprehension and as preparation for summary writing.

Most students will need practice in the introduction of a topic, its logical linked development and its register. What is best put formally in written English may be more naturally expressed using colloquial forms.

Since possibly not every student will have the chance to give a talk and also to reinforce what will have been discussed in class during such talks, these exercises might also be done in written form.

The oral exercises in Units 5, 10 and 24 are very demanding. The teacher, or a student, might stand at the blackboard to sketch on it at the instructions of the student nominated to answer the question. Any error is then immediately apparent and only an accurate description will bring a correct result. Pair work in the class along similar lines can also be tried.

Letter-writing
Some of the letters are formal. Some are informal. Every letter-exercise in the book has its own specific aim and needs its own particular register.

The exercises provide an opportunity for general letter-writing practice, lay-out, placing of address and date, opening, paragraphing, closing etc. However, students will also need practice in selecting points of information to be included, the order in which they should appear and the required register.

Most of the letters ask for a concise explanation of the text topic or a part of it. In this case many of the points listed below under *Summaries* will apply.

Summaries
Summary-writing is a very demanding exercise in comprehension and re-expression. It is valuable only if students are trained to do exactly what they are asked.

Great importance should be laid on the careful initial listing of points to be included. Individually, in pairs, in groups or as a joint class effort, students should have practice at first in making such a list, which can be discussed and agreed on before the next step is taken. Students should be directed (as in all cases of note-making) to make *brief* notes and not reproduce whole sentences from the text.

Although there can be no blanket rule against using *any* word or phrase from the original text, students should be discouraged from borrowing long extracts slightly or not at all changed to be subsequently linked with an occasional 'and' or 'but'. A lengthy borrowing usually fits ill into its new setting and often means that the student has not fully understood what has been borrowed. Emphasis should be on re-expression.

With the points for inclusion agreed on, the next step is to expand and connect them into continuous prose of the required length. Joint class efforts, guided by the teacher, are recommended initially. Students should be encouraged to write their summaries from their notes, with reference to the text only where necessary. A rough and then a final draft will normally be necessary.

Any limit on the number of words should be strictly observed. Students often take some time to appreciate the importance of the word limit. To disregard it largely invalidates the whole summary exercise.

Compositions

The composition questions usually require the student to re-express the text topic or part of it and the points made above under *Summaries* will broadly apply here also.

In two cases (Unit 9 composition 4, Unit 17 composition 1) students have to select and express information following specific models. This is to make students aware of the particular forms and registers in question.

Advertisement exercises

In four units (8, 11, 22, 26) students are asked to write an advertisement, copying the style and arrangement of one in the text. This is to make students aware of the various factors which play a part in the formation of different kinds of advertisement. They must consider the relative importance of different points of information which affect spacing, capitalization and even size of print/writing.

Register is obviously of paramount importance. Note the use of abbreviations in Unit 8, and the unabbreviated but compact style of Unit 11. Unit 22 is marked by a prevalence of passive forms, and the three advertisements in Unit 26 show widely differing approaches, with different styles and amounts of detail. Students who have had to write such advertisements will have a better appreciation and understanding of those they see in future.

Written dialogues

These exercises should ideally be done following oral practice in class. Two students at a time can be asked to act out the conversations or the whole class can be divided up to conduct them in pairs, with the teacher moving round to monitor.

Although writing dialogues is no substitute for oral practice, it goes some way towards ensuring that students are kept aware of spoken forms. Certainly the spoken forms should be insisted on, with contractions, question-tags, colloquial register and short sentences being encouraged.

In two units (7, 10) there are dialogue exercises in which the words of one person are given and the student must supply the other's. These make a dual demand. The first is that the student should find in the text the information required. The second is that this information should be expressed in a natural, colloquial form.

1 A British Rail timetable

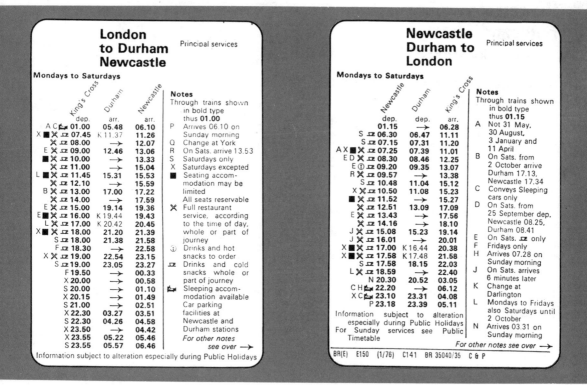

Newcastle (population about 220,000) is on the River Tyne about 250 miles from London in the North-East of England. Durham is a smaller city 15 miles south of Newcastle. The main-line station in London which serves the North-East is called King's Cross.

Comprehension

1
  a How many trains leave London for Newcastle after 5.30 p.m. on Wednesdays?

  b How many trains leave London for Newcastle after 7.30 p.m. on Saturdays?

  c Why is it advisable to reserve a seat in advance for the 10 a.m. London-Newcastle train?

  d Is it possible to get an ordinary seat on the 1.00 a.m. train from London to Newcastle?

  e Is it possible to park your car at Newcastle station?

  f Why is it advisable to check these times if you intend to travel on a Public Holiday?

  g If you want to travel on a Sunday, how can you find the train times?

  h How many trains leave Newcastle for London before noon on Saturdays?

  i On Saturdays can you have bacon and eggs on the 8.30 a.m. Newcastle-London train?

  j How many Newcastle-London trains are there with sleeping accommodation on Wednesdays?

Composition

1 (O/W) A friend wants to go by train from London to Newcastle next Saturday, leaving between 7 a.m. and 10.30 a.m. Give him or her the details of what trains there are and their advantages and disadvantages.

There are lots of ways Faresavers can help you cut the cost of travelling on the buses and tubes. See which one suits you best.

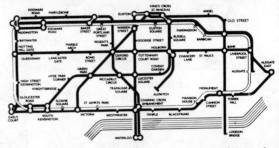

Go anywhere, any time on any red bus with a monthly Red Bus Pass

For £10.50 the Red Bus Pass gives you the freedom to use London's red buses for a month. There's no limit to the number of buses you can take or the places you can go. If you do most of your travelling by bus then this is the ticket for you. And at weekends you can take a friend for a flat 5p fare on any bus you use (except Red Arrow 500, 507).

Monthly Red Bus Passes are available from Underground stations, bus garages, London Transport Travel Enquiry Offices and agents of National Travel. The Annual Red Bus Pass is even better value and costs £110. You can buy one at St. James's Park Travel Enquiry Office or by post from the Commercial Officer, 55 Broadway, London, SW1H 0BD.

Enjoy a day out on the buses with a Red Bus Rover

This ticket is ideal for a day out in and around London. For just 90p (35p for children) Red Bus Rover takes you anywhere on any number of buses for a whole day – there are no time restrictions – and red buses cover over 1,500 miles of road. It's also great when the kids are on holiday. With one of these tickets you know they won't get stranded away from home. Buy Red Bus Rover at Underground stations, bus garages, London Transport Travel Enquiry Offices or agents of National Travel.

The Bus & Tube ticket gives unlimited bus travel to Tube Season Ticket holders

If your Tube Season ticket costs £5.30 or more a month, and you use the buses as well, then for a further £7 you can buy a Bus & Tube ticket. This gives you your normal tube season plus unlimited bus travel all on one ticket. As well as your daily tube journey you get all the advantages of the Red Bus Pass including the weekend companion cheap fare on the buses (except Red Arrows 500 & 507). Buy the Bus & Tube ticket at your local Underground station.

Save up to a third with a Cheap Day Tube Return

Remember, if you travel there and back in a day by tube at any time during the weekend or after 10 00 on weekdays you can make a big saving with a Cheap Day Return, especially on longer journeys. If the usual single fare is 30p or more, ask for Cheap Day Tube Return and save up to 33 %. Use them for shopping, visiting friends or for evening entertainment in town. And there are now special cheap fares for children too. Cheap Day Tube Returns are sold at any Underground station.

The Central Tube Rover–unlimited travel around central London for £1·25 a day

This new ticket gives you the freedom of the Underground in central London; it really puts you within easy reach of all the famous sights, museums and big stores without the headache of driving or parking. For a whole day you can travel as much as you like between any of the 49 stations on or inside the Circle Line – and we've included some other important ones just outside like Earl's Court and Waterloo (see map). Buy your ticket at any station in the Central Tube Rover area, £1.25 for adults, 50p for children under 14.

Go to work by tube and save money with an Underground Season Ticket

Let the tube take you to work and home again, avoiding the rush hour on the roads. You can buy a season ticket between any two Underground stations for a week, a month, 3 months or a year. You save about 11 % over ordinary fares with a weekly ticket; more for longer periods. And remember, you can also use your season anywhere between the same two points for extra rides at any other time; a very attractive bonus for those evening or weekend trips. Buy your season from your local Underground station.

Monthly and Annual Go-as-you-please tickets–unlimited travel on all London's buses and tubes

These tickets give you unlimited travel for a month or a year on all of London's red buses and over the whole of the Underground system (except to stations beyond Northwood, Harrow and Wealdstone and Debden). Go where you want, how you want for just £28.50 a month or £290 a year.

Buy Monthly GAYP tickets at any Underground station or at one of London Transport's Travel Enquiry Offices at the following stations: Victoria, Oxford Circus, Piccadilly Circus, St. James's Park, King's Cross, Euston.

The Annual ticket is obtainable from St James's Park Travel Enquiry Office, or by post from the Commercial Officer, 55 Broadway, London, SW1H 0BD.

Off-peak Maximum Bus Fares

Travel off-peak and the maximum fare on any bus is 22p. (For journeys outside the GLC Area 28p). And remember that children aged 5 to 15 inclusive pay only 5p on any bus inside the GLC area.

2 London Transport

The two most common means of public transport in the Greater London Council area are the bus and the underground (or 'tube'), which are operated by the London Transport Executive. The underground is usually faster and more dependable, and probably simpler for a visitor to use. On the other hand buses go to more places and they offer visitors an interesting ride and a good view. On the page opposite is part of a London Transport leaflet designed to tell people how they can save money by taking advantage of special tickets and other forms of reduced fares ('faresavers'). If you want a 'faresaver' make sure you have the latest information.

Comprehension

1   Taking what you need from the opposite page, fill in the following table to tabulate the information on London Transport Faresavers. The first one is done for you as an example.

		Means of transport	Period of validity	Cost	Restrictions on where and when you can travel and any special advantages
1	Monthly/Annual Red Bus Pass	*Bus*	*One month/ One year*	*£10.50/ £110*	*At weekends a friend can travel with you for 5p on any bus (except Red Arrow 500, 507)*
2	Red Bus Rover				
3	Bus and Tube ticket				
4	Cheap Day Tube Return				
5	Central Tube Rover				
6	Underground Season Ticket				
7	Monthly/Annual Go-as-you-please ticket				
8	Off-peak Maximum Bus fare				

2   Which 'faresavers' would suit the
     following people?
  a Miss Morton, a bank clerk, who has a
     tube journey then a long bus ride to
     work every day.
  b Mr Wall, a sales representative, who
     has to visit different places all over
     London every day.
  c Mrs Holt, who is going to visit her
     sister on the other side of London
     tomorrow. Neither of them lives near
     a tube station.
  d Mr Gonzalez, a tourist in London for
     two days.
  e Miss Blanc, a student, who has come
     to London to spend two months
     learning English and seeing the sights.

Composition

1 (O)   Looking only at the information you
        have put in your table, describe the
        Monthly Red Bus Pass, the Annual
        Red Bus Pass, the Red Bus Rover etc.

2 (O/W) You meet some tourists who have
        come to spend only a couple of days
        or a few weeks in London. Choose
        which special reductions might be
        useful and tell the tourists about them.

3 (W)   Write about 120 words on 'How to
        save money on public transport in
        London'. Use two paragraphs, the first
        beginning 'If you live in London and
        have to use public transport
        regularly. . .' and the second, 'Tourists
        who come to London for a few days
        or a month. . .'. Take your informa-
        tion from page 9, but do not include
        small details. You do not need to
        mention all the 'faresavers' if you do
        not want to.

3 London taxis

Taxis may be hailed in central London streets. When they are free the 'For Hire' or 'Taxi' sign is lit at the front of the cab.

In London there is a minimum charge of 40p for the first 900 yards, 823 metres (approximately ½ mile) of a taxi journey and prices rise by 5p for every 450 yards, 412 metres (¼ mile) thereafter. An extra charge of 5p is made for each additional passenger and 5p for each item of baggage carried on the roof or driver's platform. For hirings between 2000 and 0600 hours 10p extra is charged. This surcharge also applies throughout the week-end (day and night) from 2000 hours Friday until 0600 hours Monday. On the eight public Bank Holidays the surcharge is 20p, starting at midnight and throughout the 24 hours.

The driver has the right to refuse a hiring in excess of six miles (10 km) or one hour in duration, but where he undertakes such a hiring the fare payable is shown on the meter — no bargaining is necessary. Where a hiring is for a journey outside the Metropolitan Police District (approximately 16 miles (25 km) from central London), the fare should be one agreed between passenger and driver.

The approximate charge for a journey from London (Heathrow) Airport to Piccadilly Circus would be £5.20-£6.25.

In provincial towns, taxi charges vary from region to region, but the average charges are about 25p-40p for the first mile (approx. 1600 metres) and 15p-25p for each additional mile.

How much to tip: A minimum tip on short journeys up to 30p would be 5p and roughly 15% of the fare above that. When the driver has given any special service (e.g., helped with baggage) a larger tip is expected.

Complaints: If you have cause for complaint, report the matter without delay to a Police Officer or to the Metropolitan Police Public Carriage Office, 15 Penton Street, London N1 9PU. You should, however, take the licence number of the taxi, as any complaint is invalid without this information.

London taxi-drivers and their taxis are strictly licensed by the Metropolitan Police. Drivers have to pass a medical examination as well as a difficult test on their knowledge of London. The specially-designed taxis receive annual mechanical checks by the police. 'Mini-cabs' are unlicensed. They and their drivers are not covered by normal taxi regulations. You cannot stop one in the street. You must ring your local 'mini-cab' number.

Comprehension

1 According to the information given above, which of the following statements are true and which are false?

a The number of passengers carried makes no difference to the fare.

b You don't pay extra for a suitcase which you keep with you in the taxi.

c For every journey on a Saturday or Sunday you must pay 10p extra.

d On Bank Holidays you must pay 30p extra for every journey.

e Taxi fares in provincial towns are usually lower than in London.

2 a How do you know when a taxi is free?

b How much does a five-mile taxi journey in London cost in the middle of an ordinary day?

c About how much would you expect to pay for a two-mile taxi journey in London on Saturday for three passengers with three suitcases on the driver's platform and three on the roof, excluding the tip?

d In what circumstances can the taxi-driver refuse to take you?

e How much should you tip on a fare of £1, and in what circumstances might you tip more?

Composition

1 (O) After making brief notes, explain the system of London taxi fares, including the custom of tipping.

2 (W) Imagine you have been treated badly by a taxi-driver and write a letter of complaint, describing the incident, to the Metropolitan Police Public Carriage Office.

3 (W) Write a conversation between a person who is complaining about a taxi-driver, and a policeman. Write in dialogue form giving only the names of the speakers and their words.

SEASPEED HOVERCRAFT SERVICES
with train connections to and from London

SOUTHAMPTON—COWES

LONDON TRAINS WEEKDAYS		HOVERCRAFT WEEKDAYS	
Waterloo dep.	Southampton arr.	Southampton dep.	Cowes arr.
05 43	07 13	08 00 SX	08 20
06 46	08 11	09 00	09 20
08 30	09 40	10 00	10 20
09 30	10 40	11 00	11 20
10 30	11 40	12 00	12 20
11 30	12 40	13 00	13 20
12 30	13 40	14 00	14 20
13 30	14 40	15 00	15 20
14 30	15 40	16 00	16 20
15 30	16 40	17 00	17 20
16 30	17 40	18 00	18 20
17 30	18 48	19 00	19 20
18 30	19 42	20 00	20 20

SUNDAYS		SUNDAYS	
08 30	09 40	10 00	10 20
09 30	10 40	11 00	11 20
10 30	11 40	12 00	12 20
11 30	12 40	13 00	13 20
12 30	13 40	14 00	14 20
14 30	15 40	16 00	16 20
15 30	16 40	17 00	17 20
16 30	17 40	18 00	18 20
17 30	18 40	19 00	19 20
18 30	19 40	20 00	20 20

COWES—SOUTHAMPTON

HOVERCRAFT WEEKDAYS		LONDON TRAINS WEEKDAYS	
Cowes dep.	Southampton arr.	Southampton dep.	Waterloo arr.
07 25 SX	07 45	08 08	09 23
08 30	08 50	09 10	10 20
09 30	09 50	10 10	11 20
10 30	10 50	11 10	12 20
11 30	11 50	12 10	13 20
12 30 SX	12 50	13 10	14 20
13 30 SO	13 50	14 10	15 20
14 30	14 50	15 10	16 20
15 30	15 50	16 10	17 28
16 30	16 50	17 10	18 23
17 30	17 50	18 10	19 20
18 30	18 50	19 10	20 20
19 30	19 50	20 10	21 20

SUNDAYS		SUNDAYS	
09 30	09 50	10 10	11 20
10 30	10 50	11 10	12 20
11 30	11 50	12 10	13 20
12 30	12 50	13 10	14 20
15 30	15 50	16 10	17 20
16 30	16 50	17 35	19 05
17 30	17 50	18 10	19 20
18 30	18 50	19 10	20 20
19 30	19 50	20 10	21 20

SX Saturdays excepted   **SO** Saturdays only

FARES

SINGLE	£1.50
RETURN	£2.80
OFF PEAK DAY RETURN FROM SOUTHAMPTON Available after 10.00 Monday to Friday and any flight Saturday and Sunday	£2.15
DAY RETURN FROM COWES (07.25 and 08.30 flights only) Monday to Friday	£2.05
OFF PEAK DAY RETURN FROM COWES Available after 08.30 Monday to Friday and any flight Saturday and Sunday	£1.55

BOOKS OF TICKETS Book of 10 single tickets £10.00 (£1.00 per ticket)
Book of 40 single tickets £36.00 (£0.90 per ticket)
Book of 80 single tickets £64.00 (£0.80 per ticket)

Children: 3 and under 14 years – approximately half fare.

All services, fares and other information shown in this publication are liable to alteration without notice. Service connections cannot be guaranteed.

GENERAL INFORMATION

BOOKINGS Advance reservation is recommended.
Reservations may be made by telephone or post to Seaspeed Hoverports at:

Crosshouse Road,   Medina Road,

SOUTHAMPTON SO1 9GZ   COWES PO31 7BV
Tel: Southampton   Tel: Cowes
(0703) 21249   (098 382) 2337
or in person at the Information Office, Waterloo Station and at the Booking Office, Platform 4, Southampton Central Station.

GROUP TRAVEL
Special rates, are available for parties of fifteen and over. Details and reservations can be obtained through Seaspeed Reservations, Marine Court, Cowes. Tel: Cowes (098 382) 2303.

CHECK IN
All passengers must check in TEN MINUTES before the advertised flight departure time.

FREE CAR PARKING
Facilities are available at both Hoverports for passengers returning the same day. For passengers not returning the same day a small charge is made.

NO SERVICE CHRISTMAS DAY AND BOXING DAY.

A SPECIAL SEASPEED BUS OPERATES BETWEEN SOUTHAMPTON CENTRAL STATION AND THE HOVERPORT VIA CIVIC CENTRE BUS STATION CONNECTING WITH ALL OUTWARD AND INWARD FLIGHTS. DEPARTS CIVIC CENTRE 30 MINUTES BEFORE AND CENTRAL STATION 15 MINUTES BEFORE THE ADVERTISED HOVERCRAFT DEPARTURE TIMES (EXCEPT THE FIRST BUS SERVICE ON WEEKDAYS WHICH DEPARTS SOUTHAMPTON CENTRAL STATION FIVE MINUTES EARLIER)

BUSES
Cowes: Southern Vectis buses run at frequent intervals from Birmingham Road, close to the Hoverport, with connections to all parts of the Island.

LUGGAGE
Each passenger can take up to 30kgs (66lb) of personal luggage without charge.

HEATHROW LINK
Hovercraft/train services connect with Heathrow Airport coach link from Woking.

ISLAND TOURS
Southern Vectis operate day and half-day tours around the Island. Enquire at the Hoverport for details.

4 By hovercraft to the Isle of Wight

Cowes is on the Isle of Wight, which is a popular place for seaside holidays. The normal way to get there is to go to Southampton, on the south coast, and cross from there. Nowadays instead of going by boat, you can take a hovercraft. This is a new means of transport, invented in Britain, which can move over land or water on a cushion of air. The leaflet on the opposite page was produced by British Rail Hovercraft Ltd to give details of their service between Southampton and Cowes.

Comprehension

1   Mr and Mrs Bolton of London want to take their children Simon, aged five, and Stella, two, to the Isle of Wight for the day on Saturday. They can be prepared to leave their house at 7 a.m. and it takes them about an hour to get to Waterloo Station. They want to reach Cowes, Isle of Wight, by 10.30 a.m. in order to have a full day there.

a Which train should they catch from Waterloo?

b How much will their Southampton-Cowes return tickets cost altogether?

c Must the Boltons make reservations for the hovercraft in advance?

d Can they phone Waterloo Station to make hovercraft reservations?

e At what time should the Boltons be at Southampton Hoverport?

f How long will the journey from Waterloo to Cowes take the Boltons?

g Must the Boltons pay extra for any bags or suitcases they take with them on the hovercraft?

h If he wants to take his family on a bus-tour of the island, what can Mr Bolton do to get details?

i If he just wants to use ordinary buses on the island, does he need to enquire in advance?

j They want to leave the island as soon as possible after 5 p.m. What time should they be at Cowes Hoverport?

k On their journey back, when will they reach Waterloo Station?

l By ordinary ship the trip from Southampton to Cowes takes about an hour. How long does it take by hovercraft?

m How long will it take the Boltons to get from Southampton to Waterloo?

n The following abbreviations are used in the leaflet: dep., arr., Tel., kgs., lb. What do they mean?

Composition

1 (O)   Tell your friends how easy it is to get to the Isle of Wight from London, mentioning the main points of the train and hovercraft services.

2 (W)   After his day on the Isle of Wight with his family, Mr Bolton writes to his sister in London, who also has a family, to tell her about the day, especially the train and hovercraft services, and to recommend her to go with her family. Write the letter.

3 (W)   You have found this leaflet in a travel agency. Write to a friend suggesting that the two of you go to the Isle of Wight for a day from London. Give your friend some idea of how you will travel, times and cost.

The Post Office handles over 35,000,000 letters and 725,000 parcels every day. When around one-third of all mail is incorrectly addressed, one way or another, you can understand the sort of problems we have in ensuring that mail reaches its destination safely and quickly.

We could have difficulty reading your writing and your urgent mail could take longer than we would wish on its journey. The address might even fox us completely and we would have to return the mail to you as 'undeliverable'. That's what we want to avoid at all costs as we never like to admit defeat.

Everything you can do to give us a clear and correct address will help us speed your mail to the correct destination.

Please address clearly and correctly.

1 Name and/or title of business.

2 Number of house or building.

3 Street or road name.

4 District. Include the name of the village or district if it's not a Post Town in itself.

5 Post Town. In block capitals always.

6 County. When applicable write in full, unless there's an official abbreviation.

7 Postcode. Write it clearly in capitals as the last line of the address.

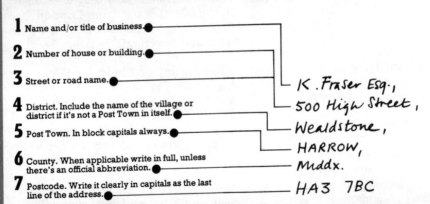

K. Fraser Esq.,
500 High Street,
Wealdstone,
HARROW,
Middx.
HA3 7BC

Your envelope should look like this.

For the best address
Some other points to watch.

Senders Name and Address: Please put your own on the back of every envelope. On parcels, write it to the left of the destination address, at right angles to it. Then if anything goes wrong it can be returned speedily and unopened.

Stamp Position: Upright in the top right-hand corner is the proper place. More than one, side by side.

Destination Address: Please write or display it at least 1½" from the top of the envelope. That keeps it well clear of the Postmark.

'Personal' Reference Numbers etc: Keep well clear of the address. Best place is the top left-hand corner of the envelope.

Abbreviations: Official ones only, please.

Window Envelopes: Recommended layouts for stationery used with window envelopes are given in British Standard 1808 Part I 1970. Particular attention should be paid to the following:

1. The panel must extend parallel to the length of the envelope.

2. No writing or printing other than the name and address may be displayed through the panel.

3. The quality of the window panel must be such that the name and address will appear through the panel so as to be read easily.

4. Enclosures must be so folded that they cannot move about in the envelope and cause the address to be partly obscured.

5 Please address clearly and correctly

A letter sent first-class should arrive at its destination the following day. Second-class mail takes a little longer to arrive and costs less. Postmen usually make two deliveries a day, except Sunday, and mail is collected from post-boxes about five times a day (twice on Saturdays, not at all on Sundays). The opposite page is taken from a Post Office leaflet.

Comprehension

1 a Did the letter shown at the top of this leaflet reach its destination?
   b Why wasn't it delivered?
   c What will happen to it?
   d How many letters a day does the Post Office deal with?
   e Why is it difficult for the Post Office to deliver all mail safely and quickly?
   f What does the Post Office want to avoid?
   g What does a clear, correct address help the Post Office to do?
   h What do you think is the purpose of the postcode?

2   According to the information given in the leaflet, which of the following statements are true and which are false?
   a If you send a letter, you should put your own address on the back of the envelope.
   b If you send a parcel, you should not write your own address on it.
   c The stamp(s) should go in the bottom left-hand corner of the envelope.
   d Stamps should not be stuck on upside-down or on their sides.
   e If two or more stamps are used, they should be next to each other.
   f There should be a space of 1½ inches or more between the address and the top of the envelope.
   g 'Personal' reference numbers should be included in the address.
   h Abbreviations should only be used if they are official ones.
   i If the envelope has a window in it, the shape, size and position of the window are not important.

Composition

1 (O/W) Without using the leaflet or drawing a picture (as if on the phone), describe to someone how you should prepare a letter for posting, remembering to mention the position of the address, the postcode, position of stamps, sender's address and other important facts.

2 (W) Write the addresses, as if for envelopes, of the Brighton Overseas Students Centre (p.26), the Secretary for Local Examination, Oxford (p.27) and the Home Office (p.62).

You should use Recorded Delivery

if your need is for a record of posting and delivery rather than compensation for loss. Recorded Delivery is particularly suitable for sending documents and papers of little or no monetary value.

What you can send All kinds of inland postal packets except: parcels, airway letters, railway letters or parcels, Railex and Cash on Delivery packets. The service does not apply to mail for the Irish Republic.

How to post Get a Certificate of Posting form from the container in the post office and follow the instructions shown on the reverse. The certificate will be your record of posting.

You must not send Banknotes, currency notes, uncrossed postal orders without the name of the payee, coin, unobliterated postage stamps, trading stamps, coupons or vouchers, savings stamps, cheques or dividend warrants which are uncrossed and payable to bearer, bearer securities, jewellery.

Handling There is no special handling in the post. Recorded Delivery mail is carried with the ordinary unregistered post: there is no special security treatment.

Record of Delivery When your letter or packet is delivered it is signed for by the recipient and a record is kept by the Post Office.
The Post Office does not undertake to deliver Recorded Delivery, or any other mail, to the addressee in person, but to the address shown.
You can obtain confirmation of delivery by completing an Advice of Delivery form (available at any Post Office) either at the time of posting or later. This form will be signed by a Post Office official — not by the addressee or the recipient. A fee is payable, which is lower if the form is handed in at the time of posting.

Compensation Limited compensation may be paid for loss or damage, but will not be paid for money or any other inadmissible item (see list under 'You must not send').

You should use Registered Post

if you want a speedy service for articles of value with extra security of handling en route, and wish to have compensation in the event of loss or damage.

What you can send Any first class letter or packet except an airway letter, Railex or railway letter.

How to post Make sure that the packet is made up in a strong cover and that it is fastened with wax, gum or other adhesive substance.
Hand the packet to the Post Office counter clerk together with the cost of postage and the registration fee. Do not post in the posting box.
Make sure that the fee paid is adequate to cover the value of the contents. The counter clerk will give you a certificate of posting which he has initialled and date-stamped.

Special security All registered mail receives special security treatment.

Packing is important: registration is not in itself a safeguard against damage. The contents of registered packets must be adequately packed.

Special envelopes Compensation will not be paid for the following articles unless they are enclosed in one of the registered letter envelopes sold by the Post Office — Banknotes, currency notes, uncrossed postal orders without the name of the payee, coin (not exceeding £5, except where the value of each coin exceeds its face value, ie. numismatic coin), unobliterated postage stamps, trading stamps, coupons or vouchers, savings stamps, cheques or dividend warrants which are uncrossed and payable to bearer, bearer securities.
These envelopes are already stamped for first class postage and the minimum registration fee, and are available in three sizes:
G 156mm x 95mm H 203mm x 120mm K 292mm x 152mm.

Record of Delivery Your registered mail is signed for by the recipient on delivery. The Post Office does not undertake to deliver registered, or any other mail, to the addressee in person, but to the address shown.
You can obtain confirmation of delivery by paying an additional fee and completing an advice of delivery form (available at any post office) either at the time of posting or later. If you require the recipient's signature on the advice of delivery, the form must be handed in at the time of posting: otherwise the certificate will be signed by a Post Office official. The advice of delivery fee is lower if the form is handed in at the time of posting.

Compensation The amount of compensation payable depends on the fee paid (see Inland Postage Rates leaflet).

6   Recorded Delivery and Registered Post

The Post Office offers many specialized services and you can pick up leaflets describing them from any post office. The leaflet on the opposite page gives details of two services which are useful if you want to send passports, money or any other important things by post.

Comprehension

1   According to the information given on the opposite page, which of the following statements are true and which are false?

a   You can send any item by Recorded Delivery or Registered Post.

b   Anything which would cost a lot of money to replace should be sent by Recorded Delivery.

c   Special packing is not required by the Post Office for Recorded Delivery.

d   If you want a Recorded Delivery certificate of posting, you must ask for one at the post office.

e   The fee for Registered Post depends on the value of what you send.

f   Registered Post is safer than Recorded Delivery.

g   A letter sent by Recorded Delivery reaches its destination more quickly than by ordinary post.

h   A Recorded Delivery or Registered Post letter will be delivered only to the person whose name appears in the address.

2   a   Describe how you get a certificate of posting saying that your Recorded Delivery letter has been posted.

b   When a Recorded Delivery letter is delivered, does the postman put it through the letter-box? What happens?

c   Does the Post Office guarantee to deliver a Recorded Delivery letter to the person whose name is in the address?

d   Describe what you do to get a confirmation of delivery.

e   If your Recorded Delivery letter is lost in the post, do you receive full compensation? What happens?

3   a   When you want to send a letter by Registered Post, what do you give the clerk in the post office and what does the clerk give you?

b   In what particular way is a Registered Post letter handled by the Post Office differently from an ordinary letter?

c   If you are going to send some banknotes by Registered Post, what should you send them in?

d   What do you do to get a Registered Post confirmation of delivery?

e   What two differences are there if you complete an advice of delivery form after your letter has been posted instead of at the time of posting?

4   Explain the following phrases by putting them into simpler English. e.g. Follow the instructions on the reverse. *Do what it says on the back.*

a   Your registered mail is signed for by the recipient on delivery.

b   The Post Office does not undertake to deliver registered, or any other mail, to the addressee in person, but to the address shown.

Composition

1 (O/W) Describe in simple English how the Recorded Delivery system works.

2 (O/W) Describe in simple English how the Registered Post system works.

3 (W)   Write a two-paragraph composition on 'Recorded Delivery and Registered Post'. Write in simple English and include only the main points. The first paragraph should describe the similarities of the two systems. The second should describe the differences. Write 70-100 words altogether.

Using the telephone

TELEPHONE CALLS AND CHARGES

Details of telephone charges can be found at the front of any telephone directory, where you will see that the cost of your call will depend not only on the duration and distance but also on what time of day the call is made and sometimes on whether or not it is made at the weekend or during the week. Between most places in Britain it is now possible to dial direct by S.T.D. (Subscriber Trunk Dialling). Charge rates are higher for calls made from coin-box phones and call offices than for those made from ordinary lines, and calls connected by the operator are normally more expensive than calls you dial direct.

S.T.D. facilities now exist between Britain and most countries in Western Europe and also with a number of other overseas countries besides. Other calls will require the assistance of the operator. Charge rates for international calls depend broadly on the same factors as for inland calls. Full details of international telephone charges and services are found in directories.

TELEPHONE SERVICES

Alarm calls, to wake you up in the morning, should be booked before 10.30 p.m. the previous evening.
Transferred charge calls are those where the people you want to speak to agree to pay for your call to them. Transferred charge calls can also be made to many countries abroad.
Personal calls are those where you tell the operator the name of the person you wish to speak to. You are not connected if that person cannot be found, though a message can be left for him or her to ring the operator later. This service is normally available for international calls as well.
Telegrams, both inland and international, may be dictated by telephone.

EMERGENCY SERVICES

From most telephones, if you want the police, fire or ambulance services in an emergency, dial 999.
Tell the operator the service you want.
Give your exchange and number or all-figure number as appropriate.
Wait until the emergency authority answers.
Then give them the full address where help is needed and other necessary information.
999 calls are free.

TELEPHONE INFORMATION NUMBERS

Current recorded information on a variety of subjects is available by telephone. The following is a selection of numbers you can phone in London.

Food Price News		01-246 8035
Gardening Information	8 a.m. to 6 p.m. each day	01-246 8000
Bedtime Stories	from 6 p.m. each night	01-246 8000
Dial-a-Disc	6 p.m. to 8 a.m. and all day Sunday	160
Motoring	information on road conditions	01-246 8021
Recipe	for an economical meal for four people	01-246 8071
Time		123
Weather Forecast		01-246 8091
Teletourist	main events of the day in and around London	01-246 8041

STANDARD TONES

Dialling tone (a continuous purring)	The equipment is ready for your call	Start dialling
Ringing tone (a repeated burr-burr)	The equipment is trying to call the dialled number	
Engaged tone (a repeated single note)	The called number or the lines are in use	Try again a few minutes later
Number unobtainable (a steady note)	The called number is not in use, temporarily out of service or out of order	Check code and/or number and call again. If again unsuccessful call the Enquiry operator.
Pay tone (rapid pips)	Instructs coinbox callers to insert money	Hold on until pips stop before speaking

FOR FULL DETAILS OF THE ABOVE AND OTHER SERVICES CONSULT YOUR TELEPHONE DIRECTORY

7 Using the telephone

Most people know how to use the telephone for local calls but have little idea of how much it costs, how to make international calls, how to use the phone cheaply and how to get a lot of useful services and information from it. You will find full details of charges and services in any telephone directory, but answer the questions below only from the summary on the opposite page.

Comprehension

1 *a* If you want to have some idea how much a phone call is going to cost, what can you do to find out?
   b S.T.D. stands for Subscriber Trunk Dialling, but what does this mean in simple English?
   c Apart from convenience what is one advantage of phoning S.T.D.?
   d Can you dial direct to numbers in other countries?
   e If you want to make an important phone call but you have no money, what can you do?
   f If you want to get in touch with someone on the phone but you don't want to pay for more than one call, what can you do? (Don't use a transferred charge call.)
   g If you are entertaining some visitors to London and want to take them out in your car, what useful information can you get by telephone?
   h If you want to prepare a meal for your visitors, what information can you get by telephone to help you?
   i If there is a serious accident in your house, someone is hurt and you dial 999, what should you say first when someone answers?
   j If your phone is in good working order, what sound should you hear when you pick the receiver up?
   k If you have dialled a number from a coin-box phone and you hear a series of rapid pips, what should you do?

Composition

1 (O/W) You must give a talk about the use of the telephone to a group of students newly-arrived in Britain. Choose from the opposite page only the most important points they will need to know and give your talk.

2 (O/W) A friend has to make a number of phone calls, inland and international, and must spend as little money as possible. Take your points from the opposite page and advise your friend how to use the phone cheaply.

3 (W)   Alice and Beatrice are in London talking about telephones. Alice's part of the conversation is given below. The spaces numbered (1) to (5) represent what Beatrice says. For each of (1) to (5). Write out Beatrice's words. Do not copy out what Alice says.
   A: I've got to make a phone-call. There's a phone-box.
   B: (1) . . . .
   A: Is it? Oh, good. I thought it cost the same. I'll wait till I get home then. Where can you find out how much phone calls cost?
   B: (2) . . . .
   A: Ah, I must have a good look. Does it give any other information?
   B: (3) . . . .
   A: Good, I'll have a look. How can I arrange an alarm call? My brother's arriving from Paris early tomorrow and I must get to the airport.
   B: (4) . . . .
   A: That seems simple enough. Actually I think I'll phone my brother this afternoon. I've got the phone number of his hotel but what if he isn't in when I phone? It could be expensive and I can't afford to keep phoning all day.
   B: (5) . . . .
   A: Perfect. I'll do that.

N.W.3. s/c c.h. lux. furn. flt. fridge ph. £26 423 7283

Hampstead Mod. cen. ht. flt. 3 rooms k. and b. tel. col. T.V. £32 inc. elec. gas 482 1266

Nr. Traf. Sq. s/c lux. furn. flt. 1st fl. 1 double bed. 1 recep. kit/diner bthrm. hall. tel. 225 6126 after 2 p.m.

N.W.2. luxury gr. fl. gdn. flt. s.c. 2 b. rec. c.h.w. & c.h. mod. bthrm. lab. sav. k. 1 min. shpg. cntre. £26 inc. 456 1387

N.W.2. Nr. tube Furn. flt. 3rd floor suit 2 sgl. sh. £24 456 2793

N.10. cul-de-sac 4r. k & b £28 754 3871

Putney. Mod. 1st fl. flt. s/c. 2 beds lnge. k. b/w.c. c.h. lift gge. no sharing £30 p.w. 894 6336

N.W.1. furn. bse. flt. 1r. bdrm. own k. sh. bth. c.h. suit prof. pers. 742 9139

S. Kensington 2 min. tube & shops pleas. furn. s/c. flt. bdrm. rec. mod k and b. sep. w.c. suit one man or m/c only min. 6 mths. refs. essent. £28 p.w. 566 2784.

W.2. Bedsit. own ckg. facs. sh. bthrm. lge. snny. rm. £14 877 7521

8 Accommodation – classified advertisements

It is obviously important to find a place to stay when you come to Britain. If you have no friends to help you, you might go to an accommodation agency, look at advertisements on cards in some shop-windows or look in newspapers at advertisements like those on the opposite page. Sometimes several young people share a flat together. It is also common to take a 'bed-sitter' or 'bed-sitting room', which is a room used as both bedroom and sitting room. If you have a 'bed-sitter' you either share a kitchen with other tenants in the house or you have simple cooking facilities in the room.

Comprehension

1
a 'S/c' means 'self-contained' (not sharing anything, independent). What does 'c.h. lux. furn. flt.' mean?

b Why needn't the tenant of the second flat worry about electricity or gas expenses?

c 'C.h.w.' is 'constant hot water'. What is a 'kit/diner' and a 'lab. sav. k.'?

d Which flat would be more suitable for an old person, the third or fourth? Give your reasons.

e Why isn't the fifth flat suitable for a married couple?

f What is the advantage of living in a cul-de-sac?

g What is a 'b/w.c.'? And a 'lnge'? And a 'gge'?

h Why can't the eighth flat be described as 's/c'? Give an example of a 'prof. pers.'

i How do we know that the advertiser of the South Kensington flat is rather particular about the tenants?

j What is a 'bedsit'? Is this a bright place? Has it a kitchen?

Composition

1 (O/W) Describe each advertised place as you would in ordinary English.

2 (W) Write a letter to a friend describing two of the above flats (only from the advertisement details; you haven't seen the flats themselves) which you think might suit you, and tell your friend which you prefer and why.

3 (W)

Tel: 722 8636

6 Rye Road,
Hampstead,
London, N.W.3.

6 October, 1977

Dear Bob,
    Sorry I haven't written for so long. I bought a new flat last March, and now I've got to go to Scotland because of work! It's a nice flat in a small block, 2 storeys (I'm at the top). I'm completely independent. I've got my own kitchen (also designed to eat in) with all kinds of gadgets and automatic things, and my own bathroom (the toilet's in it, but it doesn't matter much). The main shops and underground station are just round the corner. I've got hot water 24 hours a day. Marvellous! It's not very big. Just lounge and small bedroom.
    Now I'll have to rent it out. I'll leave all the furniture and everything of course. I think I'll ask about £25 a week and that'll include gas and electricity. I'd like a teacher, doctor or businessman. Someone quiet and serious. Do you know anyone? He or she could ring me any evening after 8.
            Yours,
            Jack

Bob couldn't help, so Jack put an advertisement in the newspaper. Write this advertisement, making it as short as possible. Do not include anything which is not in Jack's letter.

Payment of rent and giving of notice

You will usually have to pay your rent weekly in advance on a fixed day of the week. If you subsequently wish to leave you will usually have to tell your landlady one week in advance on the day of the week on which you pay your rent, but if you pay your rent monthly you will probably be required to give one month's notice. Where rent is paid for furnished accommodation, where no meals are provided, a month's notice can legally be required whether the rent is paid weekly or monthly. It is important therefore to have a definite arrangement with your landlady at the beginning of your tenancy of the exact amount of notice to be given. Similar arrangements also apply if the landlady wishes to give you notice. You may be asked to pay a deposit. If so make sure that you understand exactly what it is for: against damage (other than fair wear and tear); in lieu of notice (that is if you have to leave without giving your landlady the required amount of warning); or on the key which would be recoverable when you return it on leaving. You ought to get a receipt for any deposit and this may state the purpose. You should make sure that you have a rent book or some sort of receipt for your rent. If the landlady does not provide a rent book you are advised to get one yourself and make sure that the landlady signs it when you pay your rent. If there are 'house regulations' recorded in the rent book or displayed anywhere in the house make sure that you understand them fully as they can well be part of the contract of tenancy between you and the landlady. A single room is for the use of one person only; it cannot be shared with anyone else without the permission of the landlady. You may be asked to sign a separate agreement especially in the case of self-contained accommodation. Since this will be legally binding and will commit you to paying for the accommodation for the specific period quoted, you should study it carefully before signing it and seek legal advice if you feel this is necessary. Having signed the agreement you should make sure that you have a copy of it as you are entitled to have one.

Living in your accommodation

Be adaptable If you live in lodgings observe the customs of the household. Find out at what hour meals are served and be punctual for them; get information too about when it is most suitable for guests to visit you, when it is convenient to have a bath, and other matters in which the landlady would appreciate your co-operation. For instance, if you know you will return home late, tell her so that she can give you a key.

Be your own servant In lodgings your landlady would be glad if you helped to keep your part of the house clean and tidy and made your own bed. If you live in a flat you will have to do your own housework.

Heating, electricity, gas Gas or electricity for heating and baths is usually an extra charge in lodgings, and you will have to pay for it by means of a meter into which coins are inserted. The meters vary in type and you should ask exactly how they work. Not all private houses have central heating and bedrooms can be very cold in the winter. Make sure you have enough blankets to keep you warm. You must sleep between the sheets and if necessary buy a hot water bottle to warm the sheets before you go to bed. It is very expensive (and unhealthy) to heat your bedroom throughout the night. Gas and electric heaters need adequate ventilation and they should not be left on all night. If there is a gas fire in your bedroom make sure the gas tap is turned off before you go to bed. On no account should you blow out the flame on a gas fire or turn on the gas without lighting it immediately. Before using your own electrical apparatus such as a razor, iron or fire, make sure that it works on the voltage of the house (240 volts) and that the power point can take the power the apparatus needs; if not, you may damage your equipment or fuse all the lights. When buying apparatus be careful of secondhand goods, and only buy those which conform to the British Safety Standards.

Drinking water In any part of Britain water from the 'cold' tap is safe to drink, unless otherwise indicated - for instance, on the trains.

Keeping clothes clean It is as well to get used to washing your own clothes. You could wash small items yourself, but in lodgings and hostels you should ask whether this is allowed, and if so where things can be dried. If this is not possible you will have to send your washing to a laundry, or take it yourself to a 'launderette'. Laundries are expensive and may take a week or two to return your clothes. If you do use laundries you should make a list of any items you send, and keep a copy of the list for yourself, in case anything is lost.

There is a launderette in most areas. Students make use of launderettes since they are much cheaper and quicker than laundries. The washing machines and dryers are coin-operated. You will have to make your own arrangements for ironing. In most launderettes there is usually an automatic dry-cleaning machine, operated in the same way as the other machines, where some of your heavier outer garments can be cleaned while you wait. You will find this is much cheaper than taking coats and suits to a dry-cleaning shop.

9   Accommodation

For many students who come to Britain it is the first time they have had to look after themselves. The extract from a British Council booklet on the opposite page gives some basic advice on what you should know when you move into accommodation for the first time.

Comprehension

1   a What is the normal method of paying rent and how much notice must you usually give?
   b In what circumstances can a month's notice be legally required?
   c You should make sure what the purpose of your deposit is. Give three possibilities.
   d You should have a record of every rent payment. In what two ways can you have this?
   e Why should you pay careful attention to 'house regulations'?
   f In what particular situation might you be asked to sign a separate agreement?
   g What do you think 'self-contained' accommodation is?

2   Say whether each of the following sentences is true or false according to the information on the opposite page.
   a If you live in lodgings, you should ask your landlady about meal-times, guests and baths.
   b Your landlady will usually clean your room and make your bed.
   c Gas and electricity charges are usually included in the rent.
   d If you have to pay separately for gas and electricity, you pay by putting coins in a meter.
   e A hot water bottle is to make coffee late at night.
   f You should make sure there is a reasonable circulation of air in your room, and turn heaters and fires off at night.
   g Power points will accept electrical appliances of all kinds.
   h It is never safe to drink water from the 'cold' tap.
   i Hostels and lodgings will usually do your washing for you.
   j Launderettes are quicker but more expensive than laundries.
   k If you take your clothes to a launderette, you will have to iron them yourself.
   l Coats and suits can usually be cleaned at a launderette.

Composition

1 (O)   Make brief notes and then give a short talk to students who are new to Britain about paying rent and giving notice.

2 (O)   There are five sections under 'Living in your accommodation'. After making brief notes, give a short talk on each.

3 (W)   Make a list of the main points from the opposite page which a person will need to know as soon as he or she finds accommodation. Do not include less important details and points which a person can learn later.

From these points write a letter to a friend who is coming to Britain, advising him or her about accommodation.

4 (W)   Re-write the part 'Living in your accommodation' in the form of questions and answers like the passages on smoking on page 34, and bank accounts on page 42. Do not include all the small details but make only about 5-8 questions with answers, to cover the things that someone coming to Britain would need to know and might worry about.

do you know the wiring colours?

why the colours have changed

Most of the countries of Europe, including Britain, have reached agreement on an international standard for the colours of the wires in the flexes attached to all household electrical appliances: electric fires, electric irons, washing machines, etc.

In the past, different countries used different colours to distinguish the live, neutral and earth wires. As a result the colours used in flexes attached to some imported appliances differed from those normally used in this country, and this led to the danger of wrong connection to the plug. The new agreement has reduced this danger.

From 1st April 1971 it became a requirement in law for the cores of all 3-core flexes attached to domestic appliances on sale in this country to be coloured in accordance with the new code (see illustration below) and it is not permissible to manufacture or sell any other colours.

Some hints for connecting plugs

1. Make the connections as shown inside and make sure all the screws are tight.

2. If your flex has wires with any other colours consult a qualified electrician or your electrical shop or showroom.

3. Never use a two-pin plug to connect a three-wire flex.

4. Do not use the earth terminal when connecting a two-wire flex to a three-pin plug.

5. If your appliance has a metal case always use a three-wire flex and a three-pin plug unless the appliance is marked ▣ which means it is double-insulated.

IT IS IMPORTANT TO FIT A PLUG PROPERLY, SO IF YOU ARE IN ANY DOUBT, CONSULT YOUR ELECTRICAL SHOP OR SHOWROOM OR A QUALIFIED ELECTRICIAN

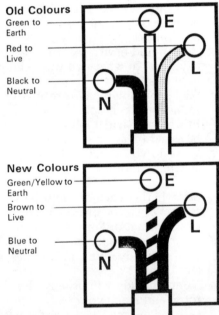

Old Colours
Green to Earth
Red to Live
Black to Neutral

New Colours
Green/Yellow to Earth
Brown to Live
Blue to Neutral

Markings on plugs
In the past, the pins of electrical plugs have been marked in many ways:

Earth
'E'; or the electrical symbol for Earth ⏚; or 'GREEN'; or the colour green.

Live
'L'; or 'RED'; or the colour red.

Neutral
'N'; or 'BLACK'; or the colour black.

In future plugs will be marked only 'E' or the electrical symbol for Earth ⏚, 'L', and 'N'.

10   Electrical plugs

Most students like to have a radio, television, record-player or tape-recorder in their room. They might need an electric fire or iron as well. One of the first things they look for in a room or flat is the number of points or sockets, to make sure they can plug these things in.

Comprehension

1 a Which countries now follow this colour code?
   b What were the dangers before the new international agreement?
   c What does the 1971 law actually say? Use your own words as much as possible.
   d 'The new agreement has reduced the danger.' Is there still a possible danger? In what way(s) could an electrical appliance with a different colour code from the new one still be used in Britain?
   e It is important to know this colour code if you use any household electrical appliances. Name three household appliances using plugs not mentioned in the leaflet.
   f What should you do if a flex seems to have wires of different colours from the new colour code?
   g A two-wire flex and a three-pin plug, a three-wire flex and a two-pin plug: which can you use (after checking carefully) and which mustn't you use?
   h What precaution should you take if your electrical appliance has a metal case?

2   Explain the following words or phrases by giving a simpler word or phrase. e.g. to distinguish
      to tell the difference between

      a imported appliances   b differed from   c a requirement in law
      d permissible   e consult

Composition

1 (O/W) Without using the leaflet or drawing a picture (as if on the phone), describe to someone how the wires and pins on a plug should look.

2 (W)   Ann has just bought a second-hand tape-recorder. She asks Bert for advice. The spaces numbered (1) to (5) represent what Bert says. For each of (1) to (5) write Bert's words. Do not copy out what Ann says.

A: Is this plug O.K.? I don't understand electrical things.
B: (1) . . . .
A: Black, green and red.
B: (2) . . . .
A: Oh, why did they change them?
B: (3) . . . .
. . . .
A: I see. Well, what do you think I ought to do?
B: (4) . . . .
. . . .
A: Right. I'll do that tomorrow. It's got a metal case. Is that O.K.?
B: (5) . . . .
. . . .

11　Learning English

BRIGHTON OVERSEAS STUDENTS CENTRE

69 Marine Parade,
Brighton, Sussex BN2 1AD.
Telephone: Brighton (0273) 68-27-47.

Principal: B. D. GRAVER, M.A. (Cambridge).

Open throughout the year
(except 3 weeks at Christmas, 1 week at Easter).

Age 17 and over.

All levels.

Minimum enrolment: 4 weeks.

General English Courses 20 or 15 hours a week. English for the Professions (business English) 25 hours a week. English Commercial Studies (supplementary course) 5 hours a week.

SUMMER　　　: Special Vacation Courses. 3 weeks: 9 August —27 August. 4 weeks: 5 July—30 July, 12 July—6 August, 2 August—27 August, 31 August—24 September. 7 weeks: 12 July—27 August. 8 weeks: 5 July—27 August, 2 August— 24 September. 12 weeks: 5 July—24 September. 20 hours a week (morning classes) or 15 hours a week (afternoon classes). English Commercial Studies (5 hours a week). All levels.

The school is on the sea front near the centre of Brighton. Numbers vary between 80 and 200. Dining-room and recreation room (television and radiogram), reading room and language laboratory. Swimming, riding, golf, etc., available nearby.

Students who want to learn English in Britain usually go either to a Local Education Authority college or to a private language school. L.E.A. colleges are normally less expensive, but private schools usually have smaller classes. Most of the good private schools are members of the Association of Recognized English Language Schools. On the left is an advertisement for a school from the A.R.E.L.S. pamphlet.

Comprehension

1　a　What is the minimum age for a student to study at this school?
　　b　What is normally the shortest time you can study there?
　　c　Is it only for general English courses?
　　d　What is the shortest period you can study in summer?
　　e　Do they have classes for beginners?
　　f　How many students study there?
　　g　Can you eat there?

Composition

1 (O)　Make some brief notes from the advertisement and give a short talk about this school.

2 (W)　Describe the main points only of this school in a letter to a friend who has asked you to find a school for him or her outside London.

3 (W)　Imagine you plan to open a school in your own country to teach your own language. Decide what your school will offer, study the ideas and arrangement of the B.O.S.C. advertisement and write a similar advertisement for your own school.

12 G.C.E.

The most important examinations for school-children in Britain, and for many overseas students who wish to obtain qualifications to enter British colleges and universities, are the G.C.E. examinations, which can be taken in many different subjects. British children take these examinations at school but many other people study for the G.C.E. in day and evening classes at colleges all over the country. The passage above is taken from a pamphlet issued by the Inner London Education Authority to inform the public about these examinations and to tell them where they can study for them at London colleges.

Comprehension

1 *a* What do the letters 'G.C.E.' stand for?
   b Who are the G.C.E. examinations held by?
   c Which G.C.E. examinations do most students in London take?
   d What do you get from Senate House?
   e What do you get from the Publications Department?
   f How many different levels of the London University G.C.E. are there? What are they called?
   g How can you get a 'Distinction' at Advanced Level in the London University G.C.E.?
   h When you have decided which college you want to attend how can you obtain details of how to join a course and how much it costs?

Composition

1 (O/W) A friend of yours in London wants to take a G.C.E. examination at an I.L.E.A. college. Tell him what steps he should take.

2 (W) Write to Senate House asking for information about the University of London G.C.E. examinations.

3 (W) Write to a college asking for details (enrolment dates, fees etc.) of their G.C.E. courses.

1 UNIVERSITIES AND COLLEGES IN BRITAIN

There are 45 universities, 30 polytechnics and about 1,000 major technical, commercial, education and art colleges in the UK. In 1973/4 there were over 251,200 full-time students in universities of whom almost 10% were from overseas, a total of nearly 276,350 students attending full-time courses in establishments of further education and about 130,270 in colleges of education.

2 ADMISSIONS OF OVERSEAS STUDENTS TO UNIVERSITIES

2.1 First Degree Courses: Application Procedure

University first degree courses in arts and sciences are normally of three or four years' duration and, with very few exceptions, students are not admitted for any shorter period of study (see para 5 Occasional Students). The academic year normally extends from October to June and is divided into three terms. Information about courses and entrance requirements should be obtained by writing direct to the university at least twelve months before the proposed date of admission. All applications for admission are dealt with by the Universities Central Council on Admissions (UCCA) to which all candidates seeking admission to a full-time internal first degree course or a first diploma course of more than one year's duration must apply. Full details of the admission procedure are to be found in the UCCA Handbook **'How to apply for admission to a university'** A copy of this handbook and the standard application form should be obtained from UCCA at PO Box 28, Cheltenham, Gloucestershire GL50 1HY. The application form must be returned to UCCA by a stated closing date, usually in December (October for Oxford and Cambridge). UCCA will continue to send application forms to universities for consideration *at their discretion* for a limited period after 15 December, but candidates are strongly advised to ensure that their application forms reach UCCA by the stated closing date to help their chances of selection. Candidates who fail to obtain a place in the initial selection period are automatically put into the 'Clearing House Scheme' in June/July when these candidates' application forms are again sent to those universities which still have vacancies.

Students from the following countries should send their application forms to UCCA via the Overseas Students Office of their own country in London - Bahamas, Brunei, Cyprus, Ghana, Guyana, India, Luxembourg, Singapore, Tanzania, Thailand, Uganda.

Graduates of a university in Britain or overseas who wish to take another *first* degree course should approach the university concerned to enquire whether it wishes them to apply direct or through the central UCCA scheme.

Transfer   It is very rare for a student who has begun a first degree course at one university in Britain to transfer to another British university with a view to completing it there, and there is no provision for the *automatic* granting of 'credit' for university studies already undertaken. Students who have already completed some university level study should make enquiries directly with the individual university.

2.2 Entrance Requirements

To be considered for admission, a candidate must show that his earlier education has qualified him to enter the course and that he speaks, writes and understands English sufficiently well. The usual *minimum* qualifications for entry to a first degree course in a university are good passes in the General Certificate of Education, the British school leaving examination - either three passes at ordinary level and two advanced level or one at ordinary level and three at advanced level. A certificate which gives admission to a university in the candidate's own country will be taken into consideration for admission to a British university, but a university may still require passes in some subjects of the GCE or an equivalent examination. **It should be noted that possession of the minimum entrance requirements does not guarantee admission.** Selection is competitive and each application is judged on its merits. The British Council offices overseas and the Schools Council, 160 Great Portland Street, London W1N 6LL, are prepared to offer advice on the acceptability of specific overseas qualifications in place of the British General Certificate of Education. All enquiries should be accompanied by a copy of the original certificate and where appropriate an approved translation.

13 Entering a university

It is difficult to enter a university and especially difficult if it is not in your own country. If you want to enter a British university, you must know what qualifications you need to have and how you should apply.

Comprehension

1
a How long do university first degree courses usually last in Britain?
b Is it normal for students to attend just a part of a degree course?
c When does the academic year begin?
d If you want information about a course at a particular university, where should you write?
e If you want to apply to enter a particular university, where should you write?
f When you have filled in your application form, where do you send it?
g If you want to enter Oxford or Cambridge Universities, what must you remember?
h If you do not obtain a place at first, what will happen to your application?
i If you already have a first degree and want to take another one, where should you write and what should you ask?
j Is it normal in Britain for a student to begin a degree course at one university and then move to another to finish it?
k What minimum qualifications in British examinations are usually required?
l Do these qualifications guarantee you a university place?
m What will a British university do about qualifications gained overseas?
n If you don't know how useful your overseas qualifications are, what can you do to get advice?

Composition

1 (O/W) Give a talk to a group of young people from different countries who want to enter a British university to take a first degree course. Advise them what qualifications they should have and what they should do. (Take your information from paragraph 2.2 only.)

2 (O/W) Give a talk to a group of young people from different countries who want to enter a British university to take a first degree course. They have already made enquiries and are satisfied that their qualifications are adequate. Explain carefully and simply the steps they must take to apply. (Take your information from paragraph 2.1 only.)

3 (O/W) A student is often asked at an interview or on an application form to give his reasons for wanting to take the course he has chosen. Imagine you are such a student, choose your course and give your reasons.

4 (W) Write a brief letter to a university stating which course(s) you are interested in and when you wish to start, and ask them to send you information about courses and entrance requirements.

5 (W) You already have a first degree from a university in your country and you want to take another first degree in Britain. Write to the British university of your choice explaining your situation, giving your qualifications and asking what you should do.

6 (W) When you apply for a university place (or a job) you normally have to write a 'curriculum vitae', which is a brief biographical sketch: dates and details in note form of what you have done in your life, especially studies and work. Write your curriculum vitae.

The National Health Service

Medical *treatment*, except for statutory charges towards the cost of medicines, dental services and spectacles, under the National Health, is free to persons ordinarily resident in Britain.

As an overseas student residing in this country you may receive medical treatment under the National Health Service during your stay. (If you are here on a short-term basis this is generally limited to any necessary treatment for conditions occurring after your arrival in Britain but you may be permitted emergency treatment for conditions you were suffering from before arriving but only if treatment cannot await your return home.) As soon as you have found somewhere to live you should register with a doctor practising under the National Health Service so that he can attend you if you fall ill. If you need advice about registering ask the warden of the hostel, or your landlady, or the local National Health Service Family Practitioner Committee, whose address can be obtained from the local post office. If you live far away from your college it is better to register with a doctor near where you live. If your college has its own Student Health Service you could register at the college instead of with the local doctor.

If the doctor you approach has room on his list and is willing to accept you he will give you a card to complete which he will then forward to the National Health Service Family Practitioner Committee. They will send you a medical card bearing your registration number and the doctor's name and address. Keep this card in a safe place since you will be asked to produce it and give your registration number if you have your sight tested or if you have dental treatment.

There are statutory charges payable towards the cost of prescriptions, dental services and spectacles. You will, for example, if you are 21 years old or over have to pay a proportionate part of the cost of dental treatment up to a maximum charge of £10 and, at present, the chemist will generally charge 20p for each item on the doctor's prescription for medicines and such appliances as elastic stockings. While sight testing is free, the charges for spectacles broadly cover their cost.

The National Health Service will provide you with advice and treatment for illnesses which occur or recur in aggravated form after your arrival in this country. If, as a student here on a short-term basis, you seek treatment for a condition (including pregnancy) which existed before your arrival, you will be regarded as a private patient and expected to pay all expenses. A bed in a hospital can cost over £100 a week and you may have to pay specialist fees. It is important for you to find out from the doctor or hospital providing the treatment whether they regard you as a private patient or are treating you under the National Health Service. There is no way in which fees paid as private patients can be refunded and if your situation is such that you may be treated under the National Health Service (as explained above) and you do not specifically want to be treated privately, you should make this clear at the start. It will be in your interest to have a complete medical check-up and X-ray before you leave home to ensure that you are in good health.

In Northern Ireland students at recognised places of study receive general medical and dental services under the National Health Service, but they usually have to pay hospital charges. In Northern Ireland also the families of married students are not eligible for health service benefits.

14 The National Health Service

You can see on the opposite page a general introduction to the National Health Service in Britain. It is taken from a British Council booklet for overseas students called 'How to live in Britain'. It is important to know how to register yourself under the N.H.S. and to know what treatment is free and what is not free.

Comprehension

1 *a* Do you pay the complete cost of medicines, dental services and spectacles under the N.H.S.?
   b Will an overseas student normally receive N.H.S. treatment for an illness which began before he came to Britain?
   c Where can you get the address of the local N.H.S. Family Practitioner Committee?
   d Are doctors obliged to accept anyone who wants to be placed on their lists?
   e When you first go to the doctor, what must you do if you are accepted?
   f What will the doctor do?
   g What will the N.H.S. Family Practitioner Committee do?
   h If the total cost of N.H.S. dental treatment you receive is £12, how much must you pay?
   i If a doctor prescribes one bottle of tablets and some sleeping pills, how much will that normally cost?
   j *Who* do you pay for prescriptions?
   k Is sight testing free?
   l Are spectacles free?
   m In what circumstances will an overseas student receive N.H.S. advice and treatment for an illness which began before he came to Britain?
   n What will normally happen if an overseas student wants treatment in Britain for an illness he first began to suffer from in his own country?
   o Why is it particularly important to know whether you are being treated as a private patient or an N.H.S. patient?
   p What should you do before coming to Britain?
   q In what two ways are students treated differently in Northern Ireland?

Composition

1 (O/W) After making brief notes from the opposite page, give a talk to a group of students from different countries either before they come to Britain or on their arrival in Britain, explaining to them the main points of the British National Health Service and how they can make use of it. (If the students have not yet come to Britain, tell them also anything they might do before coming.)

2 (W) Write a letter to a friend who is coming to Britain explaining in simple English what he can expect of the British National Health Service and telling him what he might do before coming.

INFLUENZA AND COLDS are infectious diseases. Although you cannot be absolutely sure of avoiding them, you can take precautions to protect yourself and reduce the risk of infecting others.

The germs which cause these and similar diseases spread from a sick person by being shot out in a cloud of fine spray whenever the sufferer coughs or sneezes — or even during ordinary conversation. Anyone nearby stands a good chance of being infected. Indeed, the fine droplets may remain floating in the air of a poorly ventilated room for many hours, ready to infect all who come within their reach.

bronchitis should especially be forbidden entrance. By isolating yourself you will avoid exposure to other infections when your own resistance is lowered and you may save other people catching your illness.

Infection can also be spread by soiled hands and dirty handkerchiefs. Those looking after the patient should wash their hands immediately on leaving the sickroom. Dirty handkerchiefs should be put in a bowl containing some disinfectant. Paper handkerchiefs should be burned and not used repeatedly or allowed to accumulate.

Keep Your Germs to Yourself

You may have these germs in your nose and throat without knowing it. Much infection is probably spread by people who are in the early stages of the disease but have not started to show any signs of the illness. To sneeze or cough without covering your nose and mouth with a handkerchief is not only bad manners but bad hygiene. Everyone should make a habit of covering their mouth every time they sneeze or cough.

Children should be taught to do this from infancy.

Reduce the Dangers

The first signs of influenza are headache, aching limbs and back, and shivering, followed by a feeling of feverishness and drenching sweats. You should go to bed at once, and make sure you drink large quantities — 4 to 6 pints a day — of cool liquids.

Ample fresh air is essential. Windows in the sick room should be open day and night. The bed should be placed well out of any draughts. By keeping the room warm but well aired the risk of infecting others is greatly reduced.

The number of people entering the sick room should be restricted to as few as possible. Children, old people, and those known to be specially susceptible to

Getting Well Again

Influenza normally subsides after three or four days, leaving the sufferer limp, washed out and often depressed for some time afterwards. Complications are not common in otherwise healthy people, but if you have to send for the doctor he will be helped — especially during busy winter seasons —if you send for him before 10 a.m. or ask him in the evening to call the following morning.

The Best Protection

Keep your general health up to a high level at all times with regular meals, a good mixed diet, adequate rest and relaxation.

Avoid overcrowded places as far as possible. Take as much exercise as you can in the fresh air. Ensure that the rooms you work and live in are well ventilated while occupied and thoroughly aired when empty. Sunshine is a powerful disinfectant — draw back the curtains and let in as much as you can.

Where an epidemic of influenza is due to a germ whose identity has been determined, a community may gain some protection by the use of a vaccine specially prepared from that germ. Other forms of immunisation are of doubtful value, and you should consult your doctor before using substances advertised as protectives or cures.

15 Influenza

Because of the weather in Britain influenza ('flu') and colds are the most common causes of illness. British people often suffer from them and overseas visitors even more so because they are frequently not used to them. The Health Education Council produced the leaflet on the opposite page to advise people how to protect themselves against influenza and colds.

Comprehension

1   a   Influenza and colds are infectious. How do they spread?

     b   Why is there a greater chance of infection in a badly-ventilated room?

     c   Why should you cover your mouth when you sneeze or cough?

     d   How do you know when you have influenza, and what should you do?

     e   If someone is in bed with influenza, what should you do to stop him or her getting worse?

     f   If someone is in bed with influenza what can be done to prevent others catching it? Make a list of precautions.

     g   How long does influenza usually last, and how does the sick person then feel?

     h   Make a list of things you can do to avoid getting influenza.

Composition

1 (O)   Make some notes from the leaflet and give a talk on influenza. Talk about the following things in this order: *a* how influenza is spread   *b* how to avoid it   *c* symptoms of influenza   *d* what to do if you've got it   *e* how to prevent others from catching it from you.

2 (O/W)   You are a doctor who is called to a sick child. You find that the child has influenza. Tell the child's mother how she should look after the child and how he or she will get better in a few days.

3 (W)   Using the information from the leaflet describe how you caught influenza, what you did and how you got better.

Q. "Until recently almost everyone, including doctors, thought smoking was harmless. They even said smoking was good for the nerves. So why should I stop?"

A. Cigarettes are dangerous. And medical research has now proved it.

Cigarettes are the chief cause of lung cancer which kills more than 30,000 people every year in the United Kingdom. 15,000 of them are killed before they reach the age of 65.

Cigarettes cause chronic bronchitis with its cough and phlegm, frequent chest illnesses, and disabling breathlessness. This disease kills over 32,000 people in the U..K. 8,000 of them are killed before they reach the age of 65.

Cigarettes increase the risk of coronary heart disease, one of the biggest killers in the Western World. Compared with non-smokers the cigarette smoker is about twice as likely to die of a heart attack.

People with stomach ulcers who smoke stop the ulcer from healing and are prone to serious complications.

Women who smoke in pregnancy are more likely to lose their babies or have babies with lower body weight.

Nobody could read facts like these and then say cigarettes were good for their nerves.

Q. "I am healthy. I don't smoke too much. So how can this apply to me?"

A. People who have lung cancer can feel as fit as you do until a few months before they die. By that time cancer is too far gone to cure.

People with bronchitis think it's just a smoker's cough and that the breathlessness is 'just getting older'.

People who die of a coronary usually feel perfectly well until they get the heart attack.

It is true that the more you smoke, the greater the risk, but even ten cigarettes a day are dangerous.

Q. "But we all have to die of something. So why bother?"

A. True. You could be run over by a bus tomorrow. But you wouldn't jump in front of one. Why die sooner than you need? An ordinary cigarette smoker aged 35 dies on average five and a half years earlier than a non-smoker of the same age.

One of the saddest things doctors see is someone with a family or who is enjoying a healthy life suddenly struck down with a fatal illness due to cigarette smoking.

Q. "Anyway, I've smoked for many years so it's too late to stop now, isn't it?"

A. No it isn't. The risk of illness and of dying from the results of smoking cigarettes falls away steadily in people of all ages after they stop smoking. After you've stopped for ten years your chances of keeping well will be almost as good as someone who has never smoked.

You'll lose your smoker's cough, your breathing will improve and you'll feel much fitter.

Q. "But people who stop smoking get fat. Isn't that much more dangerous than smoking?"

A. The gain in weight after stopping smoking is due to better appetite and digestion. It can be stopped by eating less, particularly of sweet and starchy foods. It isn't dangerous, for people who stop smoking have a much smaller risk of illness.

Q. "Surely there must be something to be said for smoking?"

A. Yes; tobacco smoking has increased ever since it was discovered. The habit has always been recorded as stimulating and relaxing. But never before have we been aware of the astonishing medical facts.

Not to mention that these days there are several other good reasons why you should not smoke:
1. 10 cigarettes a day cost you about £73.00 a year
   15 cigarettes a day cost you about £109.50 a year
   20 cigarettes a day cost you about £146.00 a year
   25 cigarettes a day cost you about £182.50 a year
2. Children of smokers are much more likely to smoke than the children of non-smokers. Do you want *your* children to run into all this trouble?
3. If you stop smoking, your clothes and breath won't smell of stale smoke. Your fingers won't be stained. And you'll be able to smell and taste things much better.

One of the happiest things a doctor sees is someone who has stopped smoking feeling twice as well as before and enjoying his freedom from cigarettes.

Q. "Fine, but how can I stop?"

A. If you want to prove you can do without cigarettes there's a very helpful leaflet called "How to Stop Smoking". You can get it from your local health department, clinic or the Health Education Council.

16   Why should I stop smoking?

Every packet of cigarettes sold in Britain and every cigarette advertisement has on it a Government warning, *Smoking can damage your health.* The title of the official leaflet on the opposite page is 'Why should I stop smoking?'

Comprehension

1   According to the information given in the leaflet, which of the following statements are true and which are false?

a Medical research has proved that cigarettes are dangerous.

b Cigarette smoking causes 30,000 deaths from lung cancer every year in the United Kingdom.

c Of those people who die from lung cancer every year in the United Kingdom, half die before the age of 65.

d Cigarette smoking is the cause of heart attacks.

e If you don't smoke, you are less likely to die of a heart attack.

f Cigarette smoking is one of the causes of stomach ulcers.

g Pregnant women may die if they smoke.

2   a Cigarette smokers often feel fit and well. But why is this not a good reason to continue smoking?

b Why does the leaflet say 'You could be run over by a bus tomorrow. But you wouldn't jump in front of one.'?

c Why is it never too late to stop smoking?

d Why do some people think it can be dangerous to stop smoking, and why are they wrong to think so?

e What good effects have people said come from cigarette smoking, but what bad effects have they not known?

f In what ways might your children, your appearance and your enjoyment of life benefit if you gave up smoking?

Composition

1 (O)   Try to persuade a friend to stop smoking. Use only points mentioned in the leaflet.

2 (O)   Try to persuade someone that smoking does you good. Use only points mentioned in the leaflet.

3 (W)   Write a letter to a friend describing how you have stopped smoking and how you feel better physically, financially and socially. Use only points mentioned in the leaflet.

4 (W)   Write a conversation between two people, one of whom is trying to persuade the other to give up smoking and the other giving reasons for not doing so. Write in dialogue form, giving only the name of each speaker followed by his or her words. You can use information from the opposite page.

The safety of pedestrians

38 Drive carefully and slowly when pedestrians are about, particularly in crowded shopping streets, when you see a bus stopped, or near a parked mobile shop. Watch out for pedestrians coming from behind parked or stopped vehicles, or from other places where you might not be able to see them.

39 Three out of four pedestrians killed or seriously injured are either under 15 or over 60. The young and the elderly may not judge speeds very well, and may step into the road when you do not expect them. Give them, and infirm, or blind, or disabled people, plenty of time to cross the road.

40 Drive slowly near schools, and look out for children getting on or off school buses. Stop when signalled to do so by a school crossing patrol showing a *Stop—Children* sign.

41 Be careful near a parked ice-cream van—children are more interested in ice-cream than in traffic.

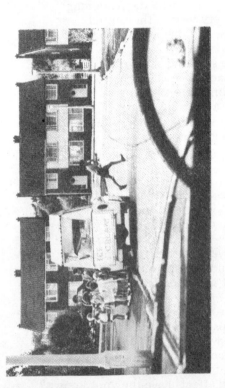

42 When coming to a zebra crossing, be ready to slow down or stop to let people cross. You must give way once they have stepped on to a crossing. Signal to other drivers that you mean to slow down or stop. Give yourself more time to slow down or stop on wet or icy roads.

43 Never overtake just before a zebra crossing.

44 In traffic queues, leave zebra crossings clear.

45 At pedestrian crossings controlled by lights, or by a police officer or traffic warden, give way to pedestrians who are still crossing when the signal is given for vehicles to move.

46 A flashing amber signal will follow the red stop signal at some pedestrian crossings. When the amber light is flashing, give way to any pedestrians on the crossing but otherwise you can proceed.

47 When turning at a road junction, give way to pedestrians who are crossing.

48 Be careful when there are pedestrians, processions, or other marching groups, in the road, particularly where there is no footpath. Give them plenty of room. Be especially careful on a left-hand bend and keep your speed down.

Animals

49 Go slowly when driving past animals. Give them plenty of room and be ready to stop if necessary. Do not frighten the animals by sounding your horn or revving your engine. Watch out for animals being led on your side of the road, and be especially careful at a left-hand bend.

GIVE WAY
to pedestrians

17   The Highway Code

The Highway Code is contained in an inexpensive official booklet obtainable from any bookshop. It gives basic advice to anyone who uses the road whether a pedestrian, a cyclist, a motor-cyclist or a motorist. If you want a British driving licence, you will have to take a practical driving test and answer questions on the Highway Code.

Comprehension

1   *a* Is this part of the Highway Code for motorists or pedestrians?

   b Why do you think a motorist should be careful near a parked mobile shop or any vehicle which has stopped by the side of the road?

   c What kind of pedestrians should the motorist be particularly careful of, and why?

   d What could happen if a motorist doesn't drive slowly near a school?

   e Why are parked ice-cream vans dangerous for a motorist?

   f If a pedestrian has stepped onto a zebra-crossing, what two things should a motorist do?

   g What two things should a motorist not do at a zebra crossing?

   h In what circumstances must a motorist not continue even when signalled to do so at a pedestrian crossing?

   i When an amber light is flashing at a pedestrian crossing what can a motorist do?

   j When a motorist is turning at a road junction and pedestrians are crossing in front of him, who may continue?

   k If there are people walking in the road, in what two situations especially should a motorist drive carefully?

   l Why should a motorist be particularly careful if there are animals on his side of the road at a left-hand bend?

Composition

1 (W)   Using the same system of short, numbered paragraphs write some instructions for *pedestrians*. Write four points only and take them from the ideas in the Highway Code on the opposite page.

2 (W)   *Using very simple English* write some advice *for children* about traffic dangers and crossing roads. Take your information only from the opposite page.

Bringing Your Car to Britain

Visitors who are members of a motoring organisation in their own country may obtain from them full details of the regulations for the import of cars, motor cycles, autocycles, etc., for tourist purposes into the United Kingdom. These organisations specialise in making tourist arrangements.

Temporary entry free of Customs charges is generally allowed for the private motor vehicle of all visitors who are normally resident outside the United Kingdom. To qualify for this concession the visitor must have spent more than half of the preceding two years outside the United Kingdom. Such vehicles are now admitted into Great Britain (England, Scotland and Wales) without production of a customs document. On arrival, visitors staying for less than six months will usually be given no document, otherwise they are given a Customs Notice (No. 115D) explaining the conditions of temporary importation and showing the date by which the vehicle must be re-exported. The notice should be kept by the visitor, as it may be required later. A maximum stay of 12 months is normally allowed under these arrangements.

The vehicles of visitors to Northern Ireland are similarly admitted without production of a Customs document.

Any bicycle fitted with a motor (e.g., 'moped') is subject to the same regulations as motor vehicles.

Petrol. Petrol prices range from about 80p per Imperial Gallon for lower grades to 84p for top grade (approximately 18-21p per litre).

Taxation. A visiting motorist temporarily importing a private car is generally granted freedom from road taxation for the same period as he is free from Customs charges, but not for longer than one year, after which he pays the normal vehicle excise duty. A Motor Licence (vehicle excise licence) in Great Britain and Northern Ireland costs £40.00 per annum, or up to £16.00 per annum for a motor cycle.

Driving Licences. A visitor can drive in Britain on a current International Driving Permit or a current domestic driving licence (which should be carried), subject to a maximum of 12 months from his last date of entry. Otherwise a British driving licence must be obtained — until you have passed a driving test you will need to be accompanied by a driver with a British licence.

Insurance. Third-party insurance is compulsory. If you intend to take a motor vehicle into Great Britain and Northern Ireland, obtain from your own insurance company an International Motor Insurance Card ('Green Card') which will cover your liability. Motorists arriving without a 'Green Card' must effect insurance with a company operating in Great Britain or Northern Ireland before being allowed to proceed – the Automobile Association (AA) or Royal Automobile Club (RAC) at the port of entry may be able to help.

Registration. A temporarily imported vehicle should have either legible foreign registration plates, or temporary British registration (which can be issued by the AA or RAC at the port of entry). The vehicle should also have the national distinguishing sign of the home country.

Purchase of Motor Vehicles. Arrangements can be made either in advance in the visitor's own country of residence, or after arrival in Britain, for the purchase of a new vehicle for use in the United Kingdom from a United Kingdom motor manufacturer (not a dealer) or from a sole selling agent in the United Kingdom of a foreign motor manufacturer.

An overseas visitor is allowed exemption from Value Added Tax (VAT) and Car Tax provided he intends to resume residence abroad for not less than 12 months and exports his vehicle when he leaves the United Kingdom at the end of his stay or within 12 months of the date of delivery, whichever is the earlier. Full details of this scheme are given in Customs Notice No. 705.

A car purchased by an overseas visitor without payment of Value Added Tax (VAT) and Car Tax under this scheme is also exempt from payment of vehicle excise (licence) duty so long as the Value Added Tax (VAT) and Car Tax exemption applies.

Motorists are advised to join either the Automobile Association (AA), Fanum House, Basing View, Basingstoke, Hampshire, Telephone: Basingstoke 20123, or the Royal Automobile Club (RAC), 83-85 Pall Mall, London SW1Y 5HW, Telephone: 01-930 4343. Both organisations provide a comprehensive service for members which includes a breakdown and patrol service, route planning, legal advice, and a variety of information and travel leaflets. Their handbooks list appointed hotels and garages throughout Britain and include touring maps and notes.

18   Bringing your car to Britain

It is very simple to bring your car into Britain if you know the few basic requirements. The passage on the opposite page is taken from a free leaflet called 'Britain: A Traveller's Guide' published by the British Tourist Authority.

Comprehension

1   Victor is going to work in Britain for about a year and he wants to take his car. It will be his first visit there. Answer his questions using simple, clear English.

  a What should I do to find out about the regulations for taking a car into Britain?

  b Will I need to show any kind of customs document when I get there?

  c I've heard that I'll be given a customs notice, 115 D. Is that true? What is it? What's the purpose of it?

  d How much does petrol cost in Britain?

  e Will I have to pay road tax, vehicle excise duty, anything like that?

  f What about a driving licence? Will I have to get a special one, or a British one?

  g What must I do about insurance?

  h Will I need to have different registration plates or can I keep the ones I have now?

  i If someone has to get British registration plates, how can he do it?

  j I might buy a new car while I'm in Britain. Who should I go to, a dealer?

  k How can I buy a new car in Britain without paying V.A.T.? What must I do?

  l I wonder if it's worth joining a British motorists' organization while I'm there. What are the advantages?

2   Explain the following phrases taken from the leaflet by putting them into simpler English.

  a They are now admitted into Great Britain without production of a customs document.

  b They are generally granted freedom from road taxation.

  c Your driving licence should be carried.

  d Motorists must effect insurance.

  e An overseas visitor is allowed exemption from V.A.T. and Car Tax provided he intends to resume residence abroad.

Composition

1 (W) A friend of yours is coming to Britain for a month's holiday and he wants to bring his car. Write a letter to him telling him the main points from the opposite page that he will need to know.

Group	Type of Car	No. of seats	Time & Mileage (1 and 2 days)		Special Unlimited Mileage Rates (rentals of 3 consecutive days and over)					
			Per Day	Plus per Mile	3 days	Extra days	7 Days	Extra days	28 days	Extra days
A	Ford Escort 1100L Vauxhall Viva 1256	4 4	£4.25	5p	£26.25	£8.75	£49.00	£7.00	£182.00	£6.50
B	Chrysler Avenger 1600 Morris Marina 1.3 Triumph Toledo 1.3 Fiat 131 1.3	4 4 4 4	£5.50	5p	£30.00	£10.00	£56.00	£8.00	£210.00	£7.50
C	Ford Cortina 1600L Vauxhall Cavalier L 1600	4/5	£5.50	5½p	£31.50	£10.50	£57.75	£8.25	£217.00	£7.75
D	Ford Capri 11 1600L Ford Cortina 1600L Estate	4 4/5	£6.95	7p	£39.75	£13.25	£73.50	£10.50	£273.00	£9.75
E	Ford Cortina 1600L Automatic Vauxhall Cavalier L 1600 Automatic	4/5 4/5	£7.75	7½p	£43.50	£14.50	£80.50	£11.50	£301.00	£10.75
F	Ford Cortina 2000E Automatic Ford Consul 2.5L Automatic	4/5 4/5	£8.50	10p	£52.50	£17.50	£94.50	£13.50	£350.00	£12.50
G	Ford Granada 3000 GXL Automatic Triumph 2.5 TC Automatic	4/5 4/5	£10.25	10p	£57.75	£19.25	£108.50	£15.50	£399.00	£14.25
H	Ford Granada Ghia 3000 Automatic	4/5	£12.50	12p	£69.75	£23.25	£129.50	£18.50	£483.00	£17.25

All rates are subject to V.A.T. Additional Hours are charged at 1/6 of the daily rate. Vehicles rented in Britain may be driven throughout Europe at these rates plus a surcharge of 25%. In all cases there is an additional charge to cover special insurance and A.A. Touring Service for Continental motoring.

TERMS OF RENTAL

DRIVERS British drivers must produce a current and suitable British Driving Licence. Overseas visitors are required to produce a current suitable licence valid in their own country. The Driving Licence must have been held for at least one year. Endorsed licences will be accepted at the discretion of Godfrey Davis. Drivers must be between the ages of 21 and 70 years (25 minimum for groups G and H). No person other than the renter or other driver approved in writing by the company is allowed to drive the vehicle.

INSURANCE Cover is provided against liability for an unlimited amount in respect of death or bodily injury to third parties and for damage to the property of third parties

PERSONAL ACCIDENT COVER Please ask for separate leaflet giving details of additional insurance cover available.

LOSS OF OR DAMAGE TO THE VEHICLE The renter is responsible for the first £45.00 of each and every accident involving any damage to or loss of the vehicle during the rental period (£80.00 for groups G and H). The renter's liability may be waived by payment of a collision damage waiver fee at the rate of 95p per day except in the case of groups G and H where the collision damage waiver is at the rate of £1.75 per day. Payment of this fee reduces the deposit from £45.00 to £12.00 plus the estimated cost of rental in each case, and for groups G and H the deposit of £80.00 is reduced to £25.00 plus the estimated cost of rental.

RATES All rates include A.A. membership, maintenance and oil, but exclude petrol. Rates shown on this tariff do not apply to rentals commencing at Heathrow Airport, London. Please ask for separate Heathrow Airport, London, tariff. Godfrey Davis reserve the right to apply minimum periods of rental without prior notice. A surcharge of 50p per day will be made on rentals of less than one week, covering Bank Holiday week-ends. Rates are subject to change without notice.

AVAILABILITY OF VEHICLES Groups A,B,C,D and E are available from all locations. Groups F and G are available at most locations. Group H is available

in London, Birmingham, Manchester and Glasgow. In the event of the model reserved being unavailable an alternative from the same or a higher group may be supplied. The rate for the model originally reserved will be charged.

EXTENSION OF RENTAL Should you wish to extend your rental beyond the agreed terminating date it is most important that the renting station is advised immediately and the required additional deposit paid so that the insurance cover is extended. Failure to do so may mean that the renter is driving the vehicle without insurance.

RENT IT HERE—LEAVE IT THERE Available from and to all the locations in the U.K., excluding Northern Ireland. Not available on Group H.

DELIVERY AND COLLECTION Available at all locations by prior arrangement. In the London area the minimum charge is £2.00 for distances up to five miles, additional miles at 12p per mile. Elsewhere the cost of delivery and collection is calculated at 12p per mile from the rental location to the delivery or collection point.

RADIO Radios are fitted in all cars in groups F, G and H.

CHARGE AND CREDIT CARDS To add to your convenience a Godfrey Davis Charge Card may be used at any of the company's locations throughout the United Kingdom. Application forms for these cards may be obtained from your nearest Godfrey Davis office. Other Charge and Credit Cards are accepted at the discretion of Godfrey Davis.

All rentals are subject to the standard terms and conditions appearing on the Rental Agreement and supplemented as above.

19   Hiring a car

Because of the rising expense of car repairs, tax and insurance, and garage rent, more and more people are hiring a car instead of buying one. There are car-hire firms all over Britain. Godfrey Davis is one of the biggest.

Comprehension

1   Keith Leach has had a driving licence for four years, since he was 20, and he's never been in trouble for a driving offence. His own car is under repair at the moment so he has decided to hire a car for a day to take his wife out. He picked up this leaflet and he has learnt that the nearest location for Godfrey Davis cars is six miles from his home in London. He wants to hire a Vauxhall Cavalier.

a How much will it cost him, without V.A.T., insurance or deposit, to hire a Vauxhall Cavalier (non-automatic) if he drives for 105 miles?

b Will he have to pay extra for petrol, or is it included in the price?

c Will Godfrey Davis accept his licence?

d Must he take out insurance himself, or will this be arranged by Godfrey Davis?

e If he pays 95p for extra insurance for the day, what deposit will he have to pay?

f If he decides not to pay this 95p for extra insurance and he has an accident which causes damage to the car costing £75 to repair, how much will he have to pay towards the repair bill?

g If the day he chooses is part of a Bank Holiday weekend, how much extra must he pay?

h Will there be a radio in his Vauxhall Cavalier?

i Will his wife be able to drive the car?

j If he wants the car brought to his house, how much will he have to pay for that service?

k If he reserves a Vauxhall Cavalier, but on the day it is not available, and he is supplied with a Ford Capri, how much extra will he have to pay?

l Could he collect his car in London and leave it at the end of the day in another Godfrey Davis location somewhere else in Britain?

m Could he hire a Ford Granada?

n Could he hire a car from Godfrey Davis and take it round Europe? If so, would he pay the same rates as in Britain?

Composition

1 (O)   After making brief notes, tell someone the principal things it is necessary to know (basic hire charge, extra costs, insurance etc.) about hiring each of the following cars. As examples of charges you can give the rates for one day and one week in each case.
a Escort   b Avenger   c Cortina (non automatic)   d Capri
e Cortina Automatic   f Consul Automatic   g Triumph
h Granada Ghia

2 (O/W) Mr Goldsmith wants to hire a car to take his family on a holiday round Britain for about a week. He wants a Granada 3000 Automatic, either a GXL or a Ghia. Write to him, or tell him, about the principal things he will need to know, such as basic hire charge, extra costs, insurance etc.

3 (W)   Taking Godfrey Davis as a typical firm, write a composition on 'Hiring a Car in Britain', mentioning only the main points and *using simpler English than the formal language of the leaflet*.

4 (W)   Write a conversation between a Godfrey Davis agent and a man who enters the office asking for details of hiring a car. Write in dialogue form, giving only the name of each speaker, followed by his or her words. Use only information from the opposite page.

- **Assuming I choose National Westminster Bank, which is the best account for everyday use?**

The most popular and practical is a Current Account. It can be opened with just a few pounds and the formalities are very simple.

- **What does a Current Account have to offer?**

You have all the safety of a cheque book service. Not only can your bills be paid by cheque, but cheques, postal orders, money orders etc. payable to you can be put straight into the account which saves time and trouble. A Current Account also relieves you of the risk of personally carrying more cash than you need as much of your shopping can be carried out by cheque. For paying into your bank account the bank supplies books containing duplicate slips, one of which you retain for your own record. You can probably arrange with your employer to have your salary or wages credited direct to your account. What is more, a Current Account is your key to a wide range of other services provided by the bank.

- **How can I find out how much money I have in the Bank?**

By enquiring at your branch. You will, in any case, be able to say how often you would like to receive your statement, which provides you with a permanent record of income and expenditure. It will show every transaction on your account and the balance remaining at the end of each day.

- **Will I get interest on the money in my Current Account?**

No. But money you may not be needing for some time can easily be transferred to a Deposit Account where it will earn interest. Normally the Bank asks for seven days' notice of any withdrawal from a Deposit Account but in emergencies you can draw immediately.

- **Can I cash cheques at any branch apart from my own?**

Yes. By making prior arrangements or using a cheque card you can cash cheques at other branches. This facility is very useful when you are travelling on business or on holiday.

- **What is a Cheque Card?**

This enables you to cash up to £30 without prior arrangement at most banks in the United Kingdom and assists you in paying shops, garages, hotels etc. by guaranteeing to the payee that your cheque will be honoured. In addition cheques up to £30 may be cashed at many banks overseas but within the Sterling Area, and, for travel purposes only, at banks in Europe participating in the Eurocheque scheme.

- **Supposing I need cash when all banks are closed?**

The National Westminster has a 24-hour Cash Dispensing Service with machines sited at a large number of branches. By using Cashcards you can obtain £10 or more at any time, day or night.

You may, of course, have a Cashcard even if your particular branch does not have a Dispenser.

- **What charges do I pay for keeping a Current Account?**

The Tariff set out below shows how you can now control the amount you pay in bank charges.

1 If the balance on your account does not fall below £50 during the charging period.
No Account Charge.
2 If the balance falls below £50 during the charging period but your account remains in credit.
a) Credit entries are Free.
b) All withdrawals are charged at 7p each **Less** an allowance of 5% p.a. on the average of credit balances maintained.
3 If your account becomes overdrawn during the charging period.
a) Credit entries are still Free.
b) Withdrawals during periods of overdraft are charged at 10p each; for all other withdrawals the charge of 7p will apply.
c) Again, these charges will be reduced by the value to the Bank of any average credit balances maintained.
d) Interest is charged on any borrowing taken.
4 Standing Orders
No additional charge.

20 Bank accounts

The National Westminster Bank produced the leaflet from which the opposite page is taken but the other British banks operate in a very similar way. Everyone who comes to stay in Britain for some time should have a bank account and should know how to use it. Banks are normally open from 9.30 a.m. to 3.30 p.m. except on Saturdays, Sundays and Bank Holidays.

Comprehension

1   a   What are the advantages of a current account?
    b   In what two ways can you find out from the bank how much money you have in your account?
    c   What is the main advantage and the main disadvantage of a deposit account?
    d   In what two ways can you withdraw money from branches of the bank apart from your own branch?
    e   Give two ways in which cheque cards can be useful.
    f   What does a cashcard let you do?
    g   When do you pay nothing for your bank account?
    h   When are you charged for your bank account?

2   The language used by institutions like banks is rather formal. Put the following phrases into simpler English to make the meaning clear.
        e.g. A Current Account also relieves you of the risk of personally carrying more cash than you need as much of your shopping can be carried out by cheque.
        It is safer to have a current account because you can pay for things by cheque instead of carrying a lot of money with you.
    a   A Current Account is your key to a wide range of other services provided by the bank.

    b   Normally the bank asks for seven days' notice of any withdrawal from a Deposit Account but in emergencies you can draw immediately.
    c   This enables you to cash up to £30 without prior arrangement.

Composition

1 (O)   Cover up the answers on the opposite page and answer the questions *in simple English* as if you are being asked by someone who has never had a bank account and you have had one for some years and know all about them.

2 (O/W) After making brief notes from the opposite page, give a talk to a group of young people on how to open and use a bank account.

3 (W)   Describe how useful it is to have a bank account. You do not need to give all the details from the opposite page. Include just the main points. Write about 100 words.

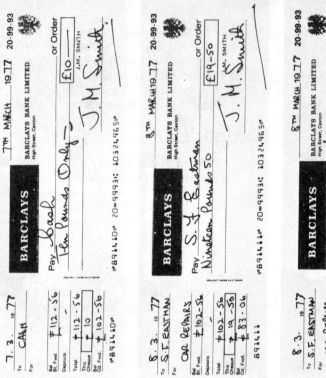

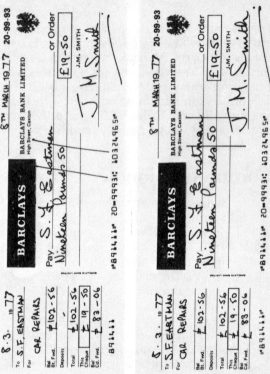

OPEN CHEQUES

This is an open cheque. A customer has completed it so that he can withdraw £10 in cash from his account.

You will see that he has made it payable to "Cash", filled in the date, written the amount he wants in words and figures, signed it, and completed the counterfoil.

Notice also that he has drawn a line very close behind the amount stated in both words and figures; and in the amount box he has written the first figure close to the £ sign. If you do the same when writing out your cheques, it will be difficult for anyone to alter what you have written.

This, again, is an open cheque, but one which a customer has completed and given to someone he wishes to pay. You will notice, incidentally, that the standard practice of rewriting the amount of the cheque in words, does not extend to the pence, and these are rewritten in figures.

Because it is an open cheque, the payee could, if he wished, take it to Caxton branch and obtain cash. But if the cheque were to fall into the hands of someone dishonest that person would also be able to cash it at that branch.

So unless you expect to be issuing a lot of cheques to people who will want to go to your branch to obtain cash for them, it is preferable, and very much safer, to use crossed cheques.

CROSSED CHEQUES

Crossed cheques have two parallel lines drawn vertically across them and are safer than open cheques because they can only be presented for payment **through a bank account.** This means they can't be exchanged for cash over a bank counter and they must be paid in as we described on page 2. (There is an exception to this rule, and we will deal with this in a moment.) If you only have open cheques then you can always cross them by drawing the two lines yourself, thus:

Whenever you send cheques by post, always ensure that they are crossed.

The cheques which we provide, and which have the crossing already printed on them, look like this:

We mentioned an exception to the rule that we don't give cash for crossed cheques. If you have a crossed cheque and want to cash it **yourself** at your branch we will do this - and in certain cases pay cash over to other people, provided that they are known to us and we are completely satisfied that they are acting on your behalf. But first you should "open the crossing", by writing "pay cash" and signing your name over the crossing

21 Cheques

The opposite page is taken from a booklet produced by Barclays Bank to explain to people who have opened current accounts (or 'cheque accounts') how to use cheques.

Comprehension

1 a On whose account are these cheques drawn?
   b What does Mr Smith want to do with the first cheque?
   c The counterfoil (or 'stub') is the part on the left with details of the cheque and the balance. This part stays in Mr Smith's cheque-book. Why do you think he completes it?
   d 'Bal. Bt. Fwd.' means 'Balance brought forward'. Where do you think Mr Smith got that figure from?
   e Why has he drawn a line after the amount?
   f Mr Smith is the 'drawer' of the second cheque. Who is the 'payee'?
   g What can Mr Eastman do with the second cheque?
   h What is the main advantage of an open cheque?
   i What is the main disadvantage of an open cheque?

2 a How can you tell a crossed cheque from its appearance?
   b How can you make an open cheque crossed?
   c What is the advantage of a crossed cheque?
   d What is the disadvantage of a crossed cheque?
   e What should you do when you send a cheque by post, and why?
   f Why has Mr Smith written 'Car Repairs' on his counterfoil?
   g Is it true that you can never get cash from a crossed cheque?
   h How can you get cash from a crossed cheque?
   i What other people can get cash from your crossed cheques?

Composition

1 (O/W) Describe the difference between open cheques and crossed cheques. Explain very simply what they are, what their advantages and disadvantages are and when each should be used.

The Wellington Museum

Apsley House, Hyde Park Corner, W1V 9FA   Administered by the Victoria and Albert Museum
Telephone 01-499 5676

Apsley House was presented to the Nation by the seventh Duke of Wellington in 1947, together with its contents. The exhibits include famous paintings, silver, porcelain, orders and decorations, and personal relics of the first Duke (1769–1852); also Canova's great marble figure of Napoleon Bonaparte. Apsley House was designed by Robert Adam for Lord Bathurst, and built 1771–78. It was bought by the Duke of Wellington in 1817, who employed Benjamin Wyatt to enlarge it, face it with Bath stone, and add the Corinthian portico (1828–29). The House was opened to the public as the Wellington Museum in the summer of 1952, and is adminstered by the Victoria and Albert Museum. An illustrated guide is on sale in the House.

TRANSPORT Bus or Underground (Piccadilly line) to Hyde Park Corner.

ADMISSION 10p Children under 16 5p Old Age Pensioners 5p
Children under 12 must be accompanied by an adult, it is regretted that no reduction in admission fees can be made for parties, but under certain conditions organised parties of schoolchildren may be admitted free of charge. Enquiries about these conditions should be addressed to the Resident Officer.

HOURS OF OPENING
Every weekday including Saturdays and Bank Holidays: 10 a.m. – 6 p.m.
Sundays: 2.30 p.m. – 6 p.m.
Closed Good Friday, Christmas Eve, Christmas Day and Boxing Day.

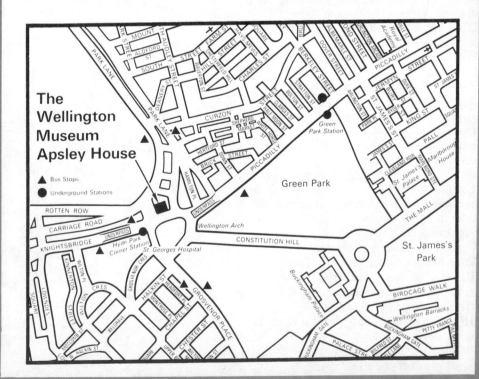

22 The Wellington Museum

Most of the museums and art galleries of Britain are free and many of them have free lectures, special exhibitions, bookshops and restaurants. The Duke of Wellington is one of Britain's most famous military heroes and is especially remembered for his defeat of Napoleon at Waterloo in 1815.

Comprehension

1 What happened in the history of Apsley House in the following years?
a 1771-78   b 1817   c 1828-29
d 1947   e1952

2 What did the following men do in the history of Apsley House?
a Lord Bathurst   b Robert Adam
c the Duke of Wellington
d Benjamin Wyatt   e the seventh Duke of Wellington

3 In each space in the following passage write the correct year or the name of the right person or place, taking your information from the first paragraph of the leaflet.
Apsley House was originally built for a . . . . between b . . . . and c . . . . It was designed by d . . . . The first Duke of Wellington, who was born in e . . . . . , bought it in f . . . . and em-ployed g . . . . to make it bigger and improve the appearance of the outside. The first Duke died in h . . . . and it was the seventh Duke who gave i . . . . and its contents to the nation in j . . . . Under the administration of k . . . . the house became l . . . . and the public was first admitted in m . . . . . .

4 According to the information given in the leaflet, which of the following statements are true and which are false?
a You can buy a guide-book of the Wellington Museum at the Victoria and Albert Museum.

b The nearest underground station is Hyde Park Corner, which is on the Piccadilly Line.
c Very old and very young people are admitted half-price.
d Adults can only enter if they are with young children.
e Children under 12 are admitted free.
f You will pay less if you go with a large group.
g School groups are sometimes admitted free.
h The museum is closed on Bank Holidays.
i The museum is open on Sundays.
j During a normal week the museum is open for 51½ hours.

Composition

1 (O/W) You are a teacher and you are going to take your class on a visit to the Wellington Museum. Tell the class what the museum is and what they will see, how and when to get there to meet you, and any other details you think are necessary.

2 (W) Write a conversation between a friend and yourself. Your friend wants to know about the Wellington Museum, what there is to see there and how much it costs to get in. Write in dialogue form, giving only the name of each speaker, followed by his or her words.

3 (W) Imagine that in 150 years from now the house where you now live in your country is famous because you became a famous person. Following the arrangement on the opposite page and making the same divisions into history, transport, admission and hours of opening, write a similar leaflet (the same length or shorter) for 'The (your name) Museum'.

WHY NOT JOIN NOW?

If you live, work, or study full time or are a ratepayer in Westminster, you may join the library free of charge merely by filling in an application form. This may be obtained from any of our libraries (see WHERE TO GO). You will then receive four tickets allowing you to borrow books or music scores up to that number. Should you require more books than this at any time extra tickets will be issued on request.

Readers who hold current library tickets of any other public library may also use the service.

BORROWING BOOKS

Twelve libraries are located in various parts of the City each offering a wide and varied collection of books for recreation, information and study. A staff of professional librarians are at hand to advise you and there is a well organised scheme to obtain books for you that are not on the shelves.

There are a number of important special collections of which the following are especially worthy of notice; medicine at Marylebone, foreign language at Mayfair, education and welfare at Maida Vale, and fine arts and English literature at Victoria.

BOOK DELIVERY SERVICE

Elderly and physically handicapped people unable to visit the library are called on regularly in their homes by a member of the staff who exchanges personal attention to their individual wants. Please let the librarian know of anyone who might be in need of this service. (Tel. 01-222 3657.)

REFERENCE AND INFORMATION

Each library has a collection of reference books selected to provide answers to general enquiries.

For more detailed information, help should be sought from the reference departments at Paddington and Marylebone or from the Central Reference Library, St. Martin's Street, which is the largest of the City's reference libraries. The collection is a comprehensive one with Commerce, Fine Arts, Theatre and Ballet being particularly well represented.

If you want to know more about the City in which you live, study or work, there are special local history departments to be found at Victoria Library (for material on the area of the old pre-1965 City of Westminster), and at Marylebone Library (for the former boroughs of St. Marylebone and Paddington). In both cases the collections include the official archives of the authorities concerned.

All reference departments are open to anyone without restriction, and enquiries on any topic, whether made in person, or by post or telephone, are welcomed.

FOR THE CHILDREN

Seven main children's libraries offer a wide range of children's books with specialist librarians to provide help and advice to children, parents and teachers. Other adult lending libraries contain collections of varying sizes depending on the demand in the area.

Extra provision is made for the under fives and parents are encouraged to join the library on their behalf as soon as children are ready to listen to stories. All pre-school playgroups and nurseries can join the nursery collection scheme and obtain a regular loan of books for use in their groups. Librarians will be pleased to arrange special sessions for visiting parties of under fives including story sessions and films.

Libraries have established close liaison with all local schools and classes are encouraged to visit and discover the wealth of books available for children.

MUSIC

Books about music can be borrowed at all the lending libraries. You will find special departments for the loan of music scores, gramophone records and cassettes at Charing Cross, Marylebone and Paddington Libraries. The record collection at Charing Cross in particular is one of the largest in the country, while the collections of books, scores and periodicals (not records) in the Central Music Library, at Victoria Library, has made it known nationally as one of the principal music libraries in Great Britain.

There are over 1¼ million books, records, cassettes, slides, microtexts and journals in Westminster City Libraries.

WHERE TO GO

Adult Libraries

Open Monday to Friday 9.30-7. Saturday 9.30-5   L•R•A•M•C (see below)
MARYLEBONE LIBRARY
Marylebone Road, London NW1 5PS
01-828 8070 ext 4036; renewals 01-935 2629;
Telex 263305

CHURCH STREET LIBRARY   L•C (see below)
Church Street, London NW8 8EU
01-262 3366

VICTORIA LIBRARY   L•A•M•C (see below)
Buckingham Palace Road, London SW1W 9UD
01-730 0446; renewals 01-730 6601
Central Music Library 01-730 8921

MUSIC LIBRARY   L•C
Rampayne Street, London SW1V 2PU
01-834 1606

ST. JOHN'S WOOD LIBRARY   L
20 Circus Road, London NW8 6PD
01-722 1960

MAIDA VALE LIBRARY   L•C (see below)
Sutherland Avenue, London W9 2QT
01-286 5788

PADDINGTON LIBRARY   L•R•M•C (see below)
Porchester Road, London W2 5DU
01-229 6611; renewals 01-229 6706

QUEEN'S PARK LIBRARY   L•C (see below)
666 Harrow Road, London W10 4NE
01-969 0543

Open Monday to Friday 9.30-7. Saturday 9.30-1   L•M
CHARING CROSS LIBRARY
4 Charing Cross Road, London WC2H 0HG
01-930 3274; 01-240 1170 after 5 p.m. and on Saturday;
renewals 01-240 3989

GREAT SMITH STREET LIBRARY   L
Great Smith Street, London SW1P 3DG
01-222 3657; renewals 01-799 2265

MAYFAIR LIBRARY   L
South Audley Street, London W1Y 5DJ
01-499 2351; renewals 01-493 7485

PORTLAND LIBRARY   L
6 Little Portland Street, London W1N 5AG
01-636 1086

Open Monday to Friday 10-7. Saturday 10-5   R
CENTRAL REFERENCE LIBRARY
St. Martins Street, London WC2H 7HP
01-930 3274; Telex 261845

L - Lending Library
R - Large Reference Library
C - Main Children's Library
A - Local History and Archives
M - Music Library

Children's Libraries

Open Monday to Friday 4-6.30; Saturday 10-1, 2-5
School holidays Monday to Friday 10-1; 2-5.30
Saturday 10-1; 2-5
QUEEN'S PARK, MAIDA VALE. PADDINGTON.
CHURCH STREET (for address see above)
Open Monday to Friday 10-6.30; Saturday 10-1, 2-5
School holidays Monday to Friday 10-5.30; Saturday 10-1; 2-5
MARYLEBONE and VICTORIA (for address see above)
Open Monday to Friday 3-5 p.m.
School holiday Monday to Friday 10-12 noon
DRURY LANE CHILDREN'S LIBRARY
120 Drury Lane, London WC2B 5SU
01-836 4225

Open Monday to Friday 4-6.30; Saturday 10-12 noon
School holidays Monday to Friday 10-1, 2-5.30
Saturday 10-12 noon
CHURCHILL GARDENS CHILDREN'S LIBRARY
131 Lupus Street, London SW1V 3EN
01-834 2849

City Librarian
K. C. Harrison, MBE, FLA

23   Public libraries

The leaflet on the opposite page describes the services offered by Westminster City Libraries in London. Every part of Britain is covered by similar groups of public libraries offering the same kinds of services and organized in more or less the same way as in Westminster.

Comprehension

1 a Who may join Westminster City Libraries?
   b How do you join Westminster City Libraries?
   c How many books are you permitted to borrow?
   d Who is permitted to borrow books from Westminster City Libraries?
   e What can you do if the library hasn't got the book you want?
   f If you are studying to be a doctor, why would you be especially interested in Marylebone Library?
   g What special service does the library provide for old people and people who cannot move about very easily?
   h Who can use the reference departments of the libraries and how can enquiries be made to them?
   i What services do the libraries offer to young children?
   j What items of interest to music-lovers may be borrowed from Westminster City libraries?

2 a If you want to renew a book you've borrowed from Marylebone Library, which number should you ring?
   b When does Church Street Library close on Tuesdays?
   c If you want to know whether Victoria Library has a certain record, which number should you ring?
   d Is Pimlico Library open on Saturday afternoons?
   e Can you borrow records from St. John's Wood Library?
   f Has Maida Vale Library a good collection of children's books?
   g When does Queen's Park Library open on Friday mornings?
   h If you want some information from Charing Cross Library at 6 p.m. on Wednesday, which number should you ring?
   i If you want general information from Mayfair Library, which number should you ring?
   j For how many hours is the Central Reference Library open on Tuesdays?

Composition

1 (O/W) As a librarian with Westminster City Libraries, you have been invited to speak to the following groups. In each case talk first about the basic library services offered and then about the specialized services offered to the particular group you are addressing.
   a The Westminster Parents' Association
   b Westminster Music-Lovers' Club
   c The Westminster Association of Old People.

2 (W) You are a student from abroad now living in Westminster. You like music and are very pleased to find that Westminster Libraries can offer you so much. Write a letter to a friend describing the services provided for music-lovers.

3 (W) Write a conversation between a Westminster Librarian and someone who has just moved into the Westminster district with his or her family, which includes a boy of eight and a girl of four. The person wants to join the library and to know about the services Westminster Libraries offer. Write in dialogue form giving only the name of each speaker and his or her words.

THE CHAMBER OF THE HOUSE

The present Chamber of the House of Commons was designed by the late Sir Giles Gilbert Scott and was opened in 1950. It replaced the Chamber designed by Sir Charles Barry, first used by the Commons in 1852, and destroyed by German bombing in 1941. The Commons acquired their first permanent home in 1547, when St. Stephen's Chapel was made available, and the chapel was used by the House until 1843, when it was destroyed by the fire which ravaged almost the whole Palace of Westminster. The lower chapel of St. Stephen's survived the fire, and is now known as the 'Crypt Chapel'. St. Stephen's Hall, through which visitors approach the Central Lobby, is on the same site and is the same size as the old Chamber.

In its shape and size the present Chamber is almost a replica of Barry's, though its decoration is less ornate, and larger galleries have been provided for visitors. The general seating arrangements of the House are in effect merely an enlargement of those in use over four hundred years ago in St. Stephens' Chapel, when Members sat in the choir stalls, and the Speaker's Chair stood on the altar steps. There are 630 Members of Parliament; but there is seating accommodation (including the side galleries) for only 437. This restriction is deliberate: the House is not a forum for set orations; its debates are largely conversational in character; and for many of them – highly specialised in theme, or of a routine nature – few Members are present, being engaged on other Parliamentary duties in the Palace of Westminster. Thus, a small and intimate Chamber is more convenient. Conversely, on occasions, when the House is full and Members have to sit in the gangways, or cluster round the Speaker's Chair, at the Bar and in the side galleries, the drama of Parliament is enhanced, and there is, as Sir Winston Churchill once put it, 'a sense of crowd and urgency'.

Amplifiers are incorporated in the woodwork at the back of each bench. If visitors lean back slightly rather than lean forward they will be able to hear more clearly.

AN ORDER FORM FOR THE PURCHASE BY POST OF THE OFFICIAL REPORT (HANSARD) OF THE DAY'S SITTING MAY BE OBTAINED FROM THE DOORKEEPERS OR ADMISSION ORDER OFFICE.

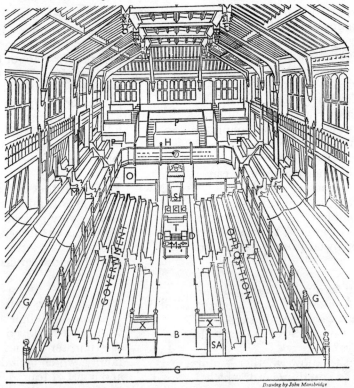

Drawing by John Mansbridge

KEY: S—Mr. Speaker. P—Press Galleries. H—*Hansard* Reporters. O—Government Officials' Box. C—Clerks of the House (when the House goes into Committee, Mr. Speaker leaves the Chair, and the Chairman sits in the chair of the Clerk of the House, which is the one on the left). T—Table of the House. D—Despatch Boxes. Ma—Mace (when the House goes into Committee, the Mace is put 'below the Table' on brackets). L—Lines over which Members may not step when speaking from the front benches. B—Bar of the House. X—Cross Benches. SA—Serjeant at Arms. M—Members' Galleries. G—Visitors' Galleries.

24 The House of Commons

Britain is governed from the Houses of Parliament at Westminster in London. The two Houses are the House of Commons and the House of Lords. The House of Commons is the more important and this is where the Members of Parliament sit, elected once every five years, or more often, directly by the people. The Prime Minister and his principal ministers (the Cabinet) sit on the front Government benches. The leading members of the main opposition party (the Shadow Cabinet) sit on the front opposition benches. On either side the M.P.s with no ministerial or other special responsibility sit at the back. They are called 'backbenchers'. The Speaker sits between the two sides and keeps order. Opposite is part of a leaflet which is given as a guide to all visitors to the galleries of the House of Commons. Anyone can go to listen to the debates.

Comprehension

1   What happened in the history of the House of Commons in the following years?
     a 1547   *b* 1843   *c* 1852
     d 1941   *e* 1950

2   According to the information given in the leaflet which of the following statements are true and which are false?
    a Barry's chamber was more ornate and had smaller galleries than Scott's.
    b The basic seating plan of the present chamber is the same as it was in St. Stephen's Chapel.
    c Every Member of Parliament has his or her own seat.
    d The insufficient number of seats was an accident in design.
    e The House of Commons is primarily a place for long speeches to be made.
    f There are often not many Members in the House of Commons.

g The House is very crowded on important occasions and this produces the right atmosphere.
h The Hansard reporters write reports of the debates for the newspapers.
i The journalists' places are behind and on either side of the Hansard reporters.
j The Speaker sits at one end between the Government and the Opposition, below the clock.

Composition

1 (O/W) Describe the seating arrangements, including the galleries, of the Chamber of the House of Commons to someone who has never been there or seen a picture or a plan of it, from the point of view of *a* someone sitting in the middle of the visitors' gallery; *b* someone sitting in the Speaker's chair.

2 (W)   After reading the first paragraph on the opposite page again, write a very brief history of the Chamber of the House of Commons in simple English. Begin in 1547 and describe the main events in chronological (time) order until the present day. Use 50-70 words.

3 (W)   Write a letter to a newspaper suggesting that the Chamber of the House of Commons should be made bigger so that all the Members of Parliament could have a seat. Give your reasons and take any information you want to from the opposite page.

4 (W)   Write a letter to a newspaper in reply to other letters which have called for a larger Chamber of the House of Commons. Support the present size and give your reasons, taking any information you want to from the opposite page.

OXFORD:
a short tour
(Shown shaded on the map opposite)

It is, of course, impossible to catch more than a glimpse of Oxford's historic buildings, gardens and rivers in a short time, but the following tour has been designed to help a visitor to see some of the chief places of interest in about two hours. The dates given after the names of the Colleges are of their foundation.

Begin at CARFAX. Carfax is the name given to the central cross-roads in the City. The tower at Carfax, built in the 14th century, is all that remains of St Martin's Church. Visitors may climb the tower in summer and get an excellent view of Oxford.

Walk down ST. ALDATE'S STREET, passing the Town Hall on the left and the Information Centre on the right. In the second turning on the right, PEMBROKE SQUARE, is Pembroke College (1624). Notice the new quadrangle created on the line of the now closed Beef Lane by the erection of the Besse Building and the adaptation of old buildings on the south side of Pembroke Street.

Cross over ST. ALDATE'S STREET to Christ Church (1525) opposite, and walk under Tom Tower with its high dome into the largest College quadrangle in Oxford, Tom Quad, with a lily pond in the middle. Tom Tower houses a bell named Great Tom, weighing 18,000 lb., and at 9.5 p.m. every day it tolls 101 strokes. This was the signal for closing the College gates to the original 101 students. To the right is the beautiful Hall (1529) containing a fine collection of portraits, with a mediaeval kitchen below. Through an archway nearby is the entrance to the Cathedral which dates from the 12th century. This is the College Chapel as well as the Cathedral of the Diocese. A passage on the north side of the Quad leads to the Library, Peckwater Quad and the Canterbury Gate.

On leaving this gate, Oriel College (1326) is to the left, and, walking along MERTON STREET, Corpus Christi College (1517) on the right is one of the smaller Colleges, with an unusual sundial dating from 1581 in its front quadrangle. A brief diversion should be made along Merton Grove, the pathway between Corpus Christi and Merton Chapel; this leads to Merton Fields and Christ Church Meadow, a green and spacious oasis between the Thames, the Colleges and the busy High Street.

Merton College (1264). This is the College with the oldest statutes. Its varied buildings make an interesting group, but the visitor should note especially Mob Quad, Oxford's oldest quadrangle, and the Library on the south and west sides of Mob Quad. The Library is the oldest in England and still keeps some of its books chained. Beyond is the spacious Chapel (1290-1450).

Turn right at the end of MERTON STREET, *and walk along* HIGH STREET *as far as* THE BOTANIC GARDEN (1621), which is one of the oldest in the country. The rose garden in front was recently laid out as a memorial to research workers in Oxford who discovered the clinical importance of penicillin. Opposite is Magdalen College (1458) (pronounced 'Maudlin'), dominated by the Bell Tower, from the top of which the choristers sing a Latin hymn at 6 a.m. on every May 1st. This is the 'May Morning Ceremony' and is witnessed by hundreds of people in the roadway or in boats on the River Cherwell below. The Chapel, Cloisters and Hall at Magdalen, all built in the 15th century, should be seen, and beyond the Cloisters, the Deer Park and Addison's Walk through the meadows. These water-meadows are another of Oxford's precious green spaces and are noted for fritillaries in the spring.

Return up HIGH STREET *to* QUEEN'S LANE. From this point the curving High Street, with its varied buildings and single sycamore tree, provides one of the best known views in Oxford. On the right are Queen's College (1341), All Souls (1437), St. Mary the Virgin Church, Brasenose College (1509), and the spire of All Saints' Church; on the left is University College (1249). This College claims an earlier origin than Merton College: some believe that King Alfred was the founder. Many of its buildings date from the 17th century. The Shelley Memorial (1894) is famous, and the Goodhart Quadrangle (1962) is a good example of a modern addition to the buildings of an ancient College.

Turn right along QUEEN'S LANE *and continue along* NEW COLLEGE LANE, passing St. Edmund Hall (c.1270), with its charming small quadrangle and new library — the ancient church building of St. Peter-in-the East, — and then reaching New College. This College was founded in 1379 by William of Wykeham who saw the first quadrangle, the Chapel, Hall, Cloisters and Bell Tower built before his death in 1404. The Chapel is famous for its stained glass and contains a statue of Lazarus by Epstein.

The beautiful garden, reached through a wrought iron gate from the Garden Quad, is remarkable for the stretch of the old city wall on the north side and the mound in the middle.

Follow NEW COLLEGE LANE *to its end, go up the steps and through* gateway opposite. On three sides are University buildings: on the right the Clarendon Building, home of the University Press from 1713 to 18 and now containing University administrative offices. On the left is Bodleian Library, and ahead is the Sheldonian Theatre built by Christopher Wren in 1664-69. The Theatre is used mainly for University ceremonies and also for concerts. It has recently been restored and time permits, a visitor should see the interior. There is a good view of spires of Oxford from its cupola.

Behind the Sheldonian is the Divinity School (c.1427-90), a perfect example of 15th century perpendicular gothic architecture, and beyond the Old Ashmolean Building (1683), housing the Museum of the History of Science.

Walk to the left along BROAD STREET. Blackwell's bookshop is across the road and next to it is Trinity College (1555) and then Balliol College (1263). A cross in the roadway opposite Balliol marks the spot where the Martyrs were burnt at the stake, Latimer and Ridley in 1555, and Archbishop Cranmer in 1556.

Turn left along TURL STREET. This is another ancient, narrow street and has Colleges on both sides. Jesus College (1571) on the right has strong connections with Wales; Lawrence of Arabia was an undergraduate here. Opposite is Exeter College (1314) which has a fine Hall built in 1618 with a collar-beam roof and a Jacobean screen. The Chapel (Gilbert Scott, 1856-59) contains a William Morris tapestry. Beyond Brasenose Lane, which still has its mediaeval middle gutter, is Lincoln College (1427) where John Wesley was a Fellow for nine years.

Turn right at the end of TURL STREET, passing the Mitre Hotel which was one of Oxford's oldest and most famous inns, dating mainly from the 17th century, *and return along* HIGH STREET *to* CARFAX.

EXTENSION OF THE TOUR NORTHWARDS

Walk along CORNMARKET STREET which runs northwards from Carfax; most of the buildings in it are modern. On the 2nd floor of No. Cornmarket Street is the 'Painted Room'. It is believed that Shakespeare slept here on his journeys to and from London. On the right, through archway, is the Golden Cross, which was an inn for over 700 years.

On the corner of Ship Street is the Church of St. Michael at the North Gate: the tower dates from the 11th century and is the oldest building in Oxford. Formerly it adjoined the North Gate of the City, above which was the Bocardo prison. From there the three Martyrs were taken to be burnt at the stake. The Martyrs' Memorial is further along beyond the next church on the right, St. Mary Magdalen.

OXFORD INFORMATION CENTRE
St. Aldate's, Oxford. Telephone 48707   Post code OX1 1DY

No. on map	KEY TO MAP	NORMAL TIMES OF OPENING.	
		Weekdays	Sundays
1.	ALL SOULS COLLEGE, High Street	2-5	2-5
2.	ASHMOLEAN MUSEUM, Beaumont Street	10-4	2-4
		Sat. 10-1 & 2.15-5	
3.	BALLIOL COLLEGE, Broad Street	10.30-5	10.30-5
4.	BODLEIAN LIBRARY, Broad Street	9-5	Closed
		Sat. 9-12.30	
5.	BOTANIC GARDEN, High Street	8-5	10-12
	Glasshouses	2-4 daily	2-4.30 or 6
6.	BRASENOSE COLLEGE, Radcliffe Square	9-dusk	9-dusk
7.	CARFAX TOWER, Carfax	Summer only	
		10.30-12.30	2-5
		2.30-4.30	
8.	CASTLE, New Road	By special arrangement only	
9.	CHRIST CHURCH, St. Aldate's	9-7	9-7
10.	CHRIST CHURCH MEADOW	7-dusk	7-dusk
	Picture Gallery	2-4.30	2-4.30
11.	CLARENDON BUILDING, Broad Street	—	—
12.	CORPUS CHRISTI COLLEGE, Merton Street	Term 2-4	2-4
		Vac. 10-6	10-6
13.	DIVINITY SCHOOL, Broad Street	9-5	Closed
		Sat. 9-12.30	
14.	ENGINEERING SCIENCE, Dept. of, etc., Banbury Road	—	—
15.	EXAMINATION SCHOOLS, High Street	—	—
16.	EXETER COLLEGE, Turl Street	9-dusk	9-dusk
17.	GLOUCESTER GREEN, Coach and Bus Station	—	—
18.	HERTFORD COLLEGE, Catte Street	9.30-dusk	9.30-dusk
19.	INFORMATION CENTRE, St. Aldate's	9-5.30	Summer only
			10.30–1.00
			1.30–4 p.m.
20.	JESUS COLLEGE, Turl Street	10-4	10-4
21.	KEBLE COLLEGE, Parks Road	10-4.45	10-4.45
22.	LADY MARGARET HALL, Norham Gardens	2-dusk	2-dusk
		(Closed August)	
23.	LAW LIBRARY & FACULTY, St. Cross Road	—	—
24.	LINACRE COLLEGE, St. Aldate's	2-dusk	2-dusk
25.	LINCOLN COLLEGE, Turl Street	2-5	11-5

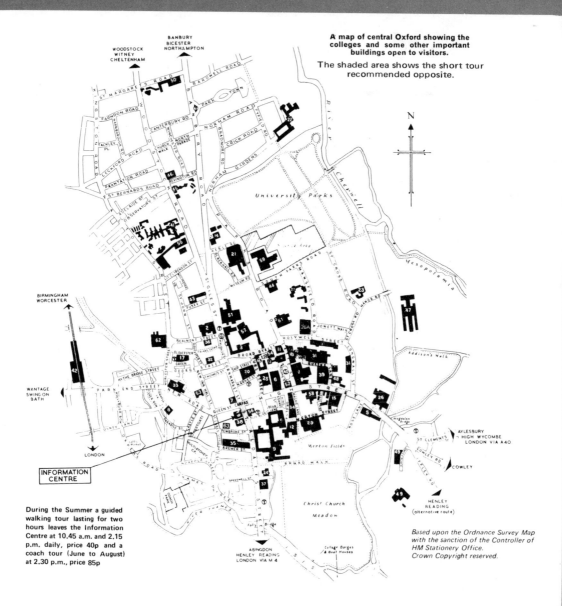

A map of central Oxford showing the colleges and some other important buildings open to visitors.

The shaded area shows the short tour recommended opposite.

During the Summer a guided walking tour lasting for two hours leaves the Information Centre at 10.45 a.m. and 2.15 p.m. daily, price 40p and a coach tour (June to August) at 2.30 p.m., price 85p.

Based upon the Ordnance Survey Map with the sanction of the Controller of HM Stationery Office. Crown Copyright reserved.

INFORMATION CENTRE

26.	MAGDALEN COLLEGE, High Street	2-6.15	10.-6.15
		July-September 10-7 daily	
26A.	MANCHESTER COLLEGE		
		Vac. 9-1 (incl. Sunday)	
27.	MANSFIELD COLLEGE, Mansfield Road	9-dusk	9-dusk
28.	MARTYR'S MEMORIAL, St. Giles Street		
29.	MERTON COLLEGE, Merton Street	10-5	10-5
30.	MUSEUM OF THE HISTORY OF SCIENCE, Broad Street	10.30-1	Closed
		2.30-4	
		Sat. Closed	
31.	NEW COLLEGE, New College Lane	Mon.-Fri.	Sat. & Sun.
		Term. 2-5	12-6
		Vac. 11-6	11-6
32.	NEW THEATRE, George Street	—	—
33.	NUFFIELD COLLEGE, New Road	9-dusk	9-dusk
34.	ORIEL COLLEGE, Oriel Square	Term 2-5	2-5
		Vac. 10-6	10-6
35.	PEMBROKE COLLEGE, Pembroke Square	10-6.	10-6.
		Term 2-6	
36.	PLAYHOUSE THEATRE, Beaumont Street	—	—
37.	POLICE HEADQUARTERS, St. Aldate's	—	—
38.	POST OFFICE (G.P.O.) St. Aldate's	9-5.30	Closed
		Sat. Closes 12.30	
39.	QUEEN'S COLLEGE, High Street	Term 2-5	—
		Vac. 10-5	10-5
40.	RADCLIFFE CAMERA, Radcliffe Square	—	—
41.	RADCLIFFE INFIRMARY, Woodstock Road	—	—
42.	RAILWAY STATION, Park End Street	—	—
43.	REGENTS PARK COLLEGE, Pusey Street	9-dusk	9-dusk
44.	RHODES HOUSE, South Parks Road	Mon.-Fri. 2.30-5.30	
45.	ST. ANNE'S COLLEGE, Woodstock Road	2-5	2-5
		Closed Aug. & Sept.	

46.	ST. ANTONY'S COLLEGE, Woodstock Road	2-5	2-5
47.	ST. CATHERINE'S COLLEGE, Manor Road	2-7	2-7
48.	ST. EDMUND HALL, Queen's Lane	9-dusk	9-dusk
49.	ST. HILDA'S COLLEGE, Cowley Place	Term only 2-5 daily	
50.	ST. HUGH'S COLLEGE, St. Margaret's Road	2-5	
51.	ST. JOHN'S COLLEGE, St. Giles Street	Term 1-5 or 7	10-1
		Vac. 9-5 or 7	10-1
52.	ST. MARY THE VIRGIN CHURCH, High Street	All day	All day
53.	ST. PETER'S COLLEGE, New Inn Hall Street	Term 2-4	2-4
		Vac. 10-4	10-4
54.	SHELDONIAN THEATRE, Broad Street	10-1, 2-5	Closed
		(Winter 4)	
55.	SOMERVILLE COLLEGE, Woodstock Road	10-5	10-5
56.	TOWN HALL, Plate Room, St. Aldate's	Tues-Sat. Inc.	
	MUSEUM OF OXFORD	10-5	—
57.	TRINITY COLLEGE, Broad Street	2-7	2-6
58.	UNIVERSITY COLLEGE, High Street	2-4	2-4
		Vac. 10-4	10-4
59.	UNIVERSITY MUSEUM, Parks Road	10-4	Closed
	PITT RIVERS MUSEUM	2-4	—
60.	UNIVERSITY PARKS (entrance from Parks Road South Parks Road and Norham Gardens)	7.30-dusk	8-dusk
61.	WADHAM COLLEGE, Parks Road	11-5	11-5
62.	WORCESTER COLLEGE, Worcester Street	2-4	2-dusk
		Vac. 9-12 2-dusk daily	
63.	MUSEUM OF MODERN ART, Pembroke Street	Tue.-Sat. 10-5	2-5
		(Fri. until 7.30 p.m.)	
		Closed Mondays	

T   indicates Toilets

25 Oxford

Oxford and Cambridge are broadly similar in age (thirteenth century), reputation, organization and size (about 10,000 students each). Only London University (over 30,000 students) is bigger in Britain. Oxford has a population of about 110,000 and is 60 miles north-west of London. It takes a little over an hour to get there by train from London. On pages 52 and 53 you see a leaflet obtainable from the Oxford Information Centre.

Comprehension

1   a   What can a visitor do at Carfax in summer?

b   'Great Tom' and 'Tom Quad' are parts of Christ Church College. What are they?

c   What are the two colleges in St Aldate's (not Linacre) and which is the older?

d   Why would a visitor want to go to the hall of Christ Church College?

e   All Oxford colleges have a chapel, but the chapel of Christ Church is something more. What is it?

f   Where is Oxford's oldest quadrangle and what is it called?

g   What are two interesting things about Merton College library?

h   What is the 'May Morning Ceremony' at Oxford?

i   There are five colleges in the High Street (Oriel College is in Oriel St). Give their names, oldest first, and the centuries of their foundation.

j   When and by whom was the Sheldonian Theatre built and what is it used for?

k   How many colleges are there in Turl St, and which is the oldest?

l   Why might a visitor be particularly interested in the church of St Michael at the North Gate and what is the connection between this place and the story of the three martyrs?

m   By tradition the part of the River Thames which runs through Oxford is called by a special name. What is it?

n   When is St Peter's College open to visitors during the university vacation?

Composition

1 (O/W) You are responsible for taking a group of people round Oxford and you decide to follow the walking tour in the leaflet. Make some brief notes on the main sights and then tell your group what they are going to see.

2 (O/W) Using the map and any other information on pages 52 and 53, give a tourist directions to walk between the following places. Give street directions and mention very briefly some of the interesting places the tourist will pass.
a Keble College to St Edmund Hall
b Balliol College to Magdalen College
c Pembroke College to Wadham College.

3 (W)   Write a letter to a friend suggesting a day in Oxford and telling him or her how you plan to spend it. Take your ideas only from the map and other information on pages 52 and 53. Imagine it is summer and pay attention to the hours of opening.

4 (W)   Write a short description in about 120 words on 'Oxford and its attractions' for a tourist brochure, taking your ideas and information only from pages 52 and 53.

5 (W)   Write a conversation between a tourist who wants to see the principal sights of Oxford and an official in the Information Centre. Take your information only from pages 52 and 53, and write in dialogue form, giving only the name of each speaker followed by his or her words.

26 Employment – classified advertisements

TYPIST/RECEPTIONIST/ TELEPHONIST

(male/female)

Small, friendly office nr. Baker St. tube requires energetic person (19+) to fill this attractive position.

Qualifications required:
- Pleasant phone manner and cheerful disposition
- expert in filing
- accurate typing
- s/h an advantage but not essent.
- good references
- 3 'O' levels inc. Eng. Language
- initiative and sense of humour

We offer:
- £2200 p.a., rising by annual increments
- 4 weeks' holiday a year
- electric typewriters
- good hours
- perks and prospects

Please apply in writing to Frank Olds, Dee Services, Breen St. London, W.1.

JON MITCHEL

Oxford Street

require

SALES ASSISTANTS

Experience desirable but not essent.

Pay £2000-£2750

Hours of work 8.55 a.m.-5.40 p.m. Mon, Tues, Weds & Fri. 8.55 a.m.-8.10 p.m. Thurs. with an option of one day off a fortnight or extra pay in lieu.

Profit-sharing scheme, 4 weeks' holiday a year. Shopping discount Subsidised dng.-rm.

Applicants (m or f) please call, write or phone:

Mr Dunn, Staff Manager, Jon Mitchel, Oxford St., W.1. 01-625 2411 Ext. 281

SALES REPRESENTATIVE

Electronics Equipment

We are looking for a bright, young (25-35) person to join our dynamic sales team in selling our products in U.K. and abroad.

Applicants must have sales experience with major store groups, wholesalers and cash-and-carry outlets. Car provided, clean driving licence essential.

Salary plus commission should be in excess of £4000 p.a. Generous company benefits and unlimited prospects.

Write or call for immediate interview: ELEX Co, 68 Elond St, London, EC4. Phone 01-208 8367

Normally students who come to Britain to study are not expected to work and permission is difficult or impossible to get. However, if your situation makes it possible, the most common way to find work is to look in newspapers at classified advertisements like those above.

Composition

1 (W) Write a letter applying for one of the three jobs advertised.

2 (W) Write a reference for someone you know who has applied for one of the three jobs advertised.

3 (W) Imagine you have applied for and got the job advertised by *either* Dee Services *or* Jon Mitchel. Write a composition describing your first week in the new job, mentioning as many details in the advertisement as possible and no details not in the advertisement.

4 (W) Write an interview between an applicant for one of the three jobs and the person who is doing the interviewing. At the beginning the interviewer will ask questions relating to the requirements mentioned in the advertisement. At the end the applicant will have some questions to ask about points which are not made clear in the advertisement. Write in dialogue form, giving only the name of each speaker followed by his or her words.

5 (W) Write a job advertisement for a British newspaper describing the job *you* would like and requiring qualities and qualifications *you* have.

6 (W) Write a job advertisement for a British newspaper requiring *a* an assistant in a supermarket; *b* a waiter or waitress in a **restaurant**; *c* a sales manager for a large firm; *d* a translator or interpreter; *e* an air steward or hostess.

This leaflet provides general guidance for girls who come to this country 'au pair' and for their hostesses. 'Au pair' arrangements are the responsibility of the two parties and are not made through official channels. To remove possible misunderstandings, however, the Home Office has prepared this outline of the principles which should govern the relationship between the two parties and of the conditions under which 'au pair' girls may be admitted to the United Kingdom for a limited period.

General

'Au pair' is an arrangement under which a girl who is not less than seventeen years old comes to the United Kingdom primarily to learn the English language and to live for a while as a member of a resident English-speaking family. She receives her keep, entertainment and pocket money (£5 to £7 a week is not unreasonable) and is expected to help with the housework and the care of any children. The relationship between the girl and her hostess is a personal one depending for its success both on the willingness of the hostess to help the girl in her studies and recreation, and on the readiness of the girl to play her part in the life of the household. (The arrangements should not be confused with regular domestic employment for which, except for EEC nationals, a permit from the Department of Employment is required.)

The household and family

It is important that the hostess should give the girl full information about the household and family: she should make it clear what advantages are offered to the girl, and what is expected from her. Wherever practicable this information should be given before the girl leaves her own country; but failing that, the hostess should ensure that the girl is given all the necessary information as soon as possible after her arrival.

Information about the household and family should include a description of the house and should indicate the number and relationship of its occupants, and of any domestic help employed. It should be made clear whether the hostess is normally at home during the greater part of the day, or is regularly absent, e.g., in employment.

Study

The 'au pair' girl should be told what facilities will be afforded her for learning English at part-time classes, or under private tuition, and about the amount of time she may expect to be able to set aside each day for study and recreation.

Duties and recreation

The reasonable maximum time during which an 'au pair' guest may be expected to perform domestic tasks, or to be on call for household duties (including baby sitting and the care of children) is about five hours daily; and she should be given at least a day a week free. It is important that the 'free time' should be genuinely free, that the girl should be at liberty to meet her friends and to go sight-seeing and to concerts, cinemas, etc., and that she should have the time and opportunity for religious observance.

In return for hospitality and keep, an 'au pair' girl is expected to help her hostess with household duties on a partnership basis, and to do her share of any kind of housework which the hostess herself undertakes. Where however the hostess employs other help for the heavier chores, she should expect the 'au pair' girl only to help with such jobs as bed making, washing up, tidying and dusting, baby sitting, taking children to and from school and looking after them in the house; she should not in that case be asked to do heavy housework.

Family relationships

The 'au pair' guest will normally expect a bedroom to herself. She should be treated as a daughter of the house, taking her meals with the family and sharing their amusements. Under a proper 'au pair' arrangement the relationship between the hostess and the girl involves acceptance of social equality and is not founded on a mistress-servant basis. It follows that the girl is expected to observe the customs and way of life of the household, and to respect the authority of host and hostess.

Travelling

Where the 'au pair' arrangement is made with a girl who is still abroad, she should be given precise travelling directions and should wherever possible be met on arrival.

An 'au pair' girl will usually pay her own fares, but if she leaves a household without another post in prospect the hostess should inquire whether she has the means to return home; if not, she should be put in touch with her Consulate or High Commission.

Insurance

A girl staying here on an 'au pair' basis is not liable to pay contributions under the Social Security Act 1975 although she may do so voluntarily if she wishes. It may be to her advantage to do so if, for example, she has come from a country which has a reciprocal agreement on social security with the United Kingdom which enables contributions under both countries' schemes to be combined for benefit purposes. It is advisable for the hostess and the girl herself to consult the local office of the Department of Health and Social Security if there is any doubt about the position.

27 Au pair

One permitted employment which an overseas student, usually girls but occasionally young men, may take is as an *au pair*. An *au pair* lives with a family and helps with children and housework in return for bed, board, pocket-money and some free time. Many girls prefer to know the family well before becoming an *au pair* with them, otherwise there can be problems and misunderstandings on both sides.

Comprehension

1   a What is an *au pair* girl?
    b What is the purpose of this leaflet?
    c What makes a hostess- *au pair* girl relationship successful?
    d What should a hostess tell her *au pair* girl as soon as possible?
    e How many hours' work should an *au pair* girl be expected to do and what free time should she have?
    f What kind of work do you think an *au pair* girl should normally be expected to do?
    g In what circumstances should an *au pair* girl not be expected to do heavy housework?
    h What should the relationship be between the *au pair* girl and her host family?
    i What are the hostess's obligations concerning the girl's journey to Britain and her departure at the end of her stay?
    j Should an *au pair* girl pay Social Security contributions?

Composition

1 (O/W) Give a talk to a group of girls who have come to Britain to be *au pairs*. Use only information from the opposite page and tell the girls what they should be expected to do, what they should expect to be done for them and anything else which you think is important.

2 (O/W) Give a talk to a group of ladies who are going to have *au pair* girls for the first time. Use only information from the opposite page and tell the ladies how they should treat their *au pairs*, what they can expect the girls to do and anything else which you think is important.

3 (W)   You have seen an advertisement for an *au pair* girl to help in the house and help look after two young children. Write to the lady telling her that you are interested, describing yourself briefly and asking for more details of the work the *au pair* girl will be expected to do and of the two children. Ask any questions you have about free time, a chance to learn English, where the house is etc.

4 (W)   You have been in correspondence with a lady about an *au pair* job. You are satisfied with the conditions of the job and the lady wants you to take it. Write from Britain or abroad accepting the job, telling her when and how you will arrive and saying whether or not you want to be met.

5 (W)   Write a conversation between a lady and a girl who has come to see her about an *au pair* job. At the beginning the lady will ask the girl questions about herself and then the girl will ask the lady questions about the job, the living conditions and anything else she wants to know. Write in dialogue form giving only the name of each speaker followed by her words.

Your national insurance contributions

Why you need national insurance

In general everyone in Britain who reaches school-leaving age must be registered for national insurance. This is a compulsory state-run scheme of which, in return for regular weekly or monthly contributions, will pay you cash benefits if you are sick, unemployed, injured at work or – if you are a woman – when you have a baby. Your contributions will also pay for retirement and widows' pensions and a number of other benefits. But only a small proportion of your contributions goes towards the cost of the National Health Service: this is paid for mainly out of taxes.

There are a number of "classes" of national insurance contributions. If you are an employee and your employer will normally both have to pay Class 1 contributions. Your employer will deduct your contribution from your earnings, along with your income tax (if you pay any). If you are self-employed you will normally have to pay Class 2 and, perhaps, Class 4 contributions; and you will be responsible for paying your own contributions. Finally there are Class 3 contributions which are voluntary and which you might wish to pay in special circumstances. All these classes are dealt with on the following pages, but if you need more detailed information get one of the special leaflets from a local Social Security office.

If you work for an employer

You and your employer must pay Class 1 contributions if:
● you have reached the earliest date at which you are allowed to leave school; and
● you earn £15 a week or more (the lower earnings limit – see below).

These contributions are earnings-related, so the more you earn the higher your contributions will be although there is an upper earnings limit (above which no further contributions are due – see below). The contribution is a percentage of your earnings up to the upper earnings limit and is the same for both men and women. Special arrangements for some married women and widows to forego some benefits and pay less in contributions are described in leaflets NI 1 (married women), NI 51 (widows) or NI 51C (widows entitled to an age-related widow's pension).

Your employer is responsible for paying the contribution but can deduct your share from your earnings before you are paid. Your contributions are recorded on a deduction card and are collected by Inland Revenue, along with any income tax you may be paying through the Pay As You Earn (PAYE) system.

If you are self-employed

You must pay Class 2 contributions if you work for yourself rather than for an employer. Class 2 contributions are "flat-rate", that is they are the same whatever you earn. They are paid by sticking stamps on to a national insurance stamp card or, if you prefer, by direct debit of your bank or National Giro account.

Voluntary contributions

Class 3 contributions are voluntary and you can only pay them if you have not paid enough Class 1 or Class 2 contributions to qualify for certain benefits. Like Class 2 contributions they are flat-rate and, if they are the only contributions you expect to pay in any year, they may be paid by sticking stamps onto a national insurance stamp card. If you prefer, you can pay by direct debit of your bank or National Giro account. If you expect to pay some Class 1 or Class 2 contributions during the tax year you can pay in a lump sum at the end of the year. There are time limits within which Class 3 contributions must be paid if they are to count for benefits; and specially extended time limits for students for retirement pension and widows' benefits purposes.

Contribution rates

You can always get the current rates by asking your local Social Security office for a copy of the latest edition of leaflet NI 208.

Class 1 (employees') rates

Employer	10.75%	of employee's earnings
Employee: (standard rate)	5.75%	
Employee: (reduced rate)	2%	
Lower earnings limit	£15 a week	
Upper earnings limit	£105 a week	

Class 2 (self-employed) rates

Men	£2.66 a week
Women	£2.55 a week
Small earnings limit below which you can apply not to pay contributions	£875 a year

Class 3 (voluntary) rate . . . . £2.45 a week

Class 4 rate . . . . .8% of profits or gains
Profits or gains on which contributions are calculated . . . . £1750 to £5500 a year

28 National insurance

Britain is a 'welfare state', that is a state which believes in providing services for its people from birth to death. Free education, grants for students, free or cheap medical services, unemployment benefits and old age pensions are examples of services found in a welfare state. But of course the money must come from somewhere. Opposite is a brief extract from a leaflet on Social Security issued by the Department of Health and Social Security.

Comprehension

1 a Who should be registered for national insurance?
b What is the purpose of national insurance, and how does it work?
c What is the relationship between national insurance contributions and the National Health Service?
d If you are employed by someone, how is your national insurance contribution made?
e If you are self-employed, how is your national insurance contribution made?
f How much is your national insurance contribution if you are employed by someone?
g Who collects your national insurance contribution and what else do they collect?
h How much is your national insurance contribution if you are self-employed?
i Why would someone want to pay Class 3 contributions, how much are they and how are they paid?

2 Explain the following phrases taken from the leaflet by putting them into simpler English.
a This is a compulsory state-run scheme.
b These contributions are earnings-related.
c to forego some benefits and pay less in contributions.
d Widows entitled to an age-related widow's pension.
e He can deduct your share before you are paid.
f Class 2 contributions are flat-rate.
g You can pay in a lump sum.

Composition

1 (O) After making brief notes give a short talk on a an employed person's national insurance contributions b a self-employed person's national insurance contributions c national insurance contributions.

2 (W) Write a composition on 'National Insurance Contributions in Britain', explaining the purpose of the system and how it works.

The Sex Discrimination Act came into force on 29 December 1975.

This leaflet briefly describes your rights, how they may affect you and where you may get detailed information.

To reflect the realities of discrimination, this leaflet refers to the victim of unfair treatment as a woman, although the law equally protects a man.

It is now unlawful to treat anyone, on the grounds of sex, less favourably than a person of the opposite sex is or would be treated in the same circumstances. Sex discrimination is not allowed in:

Employment
Education
The provision of housing, goods, facilities and services
Advertising

In Employment, it is also unlawful to discriminate because a person is married.

Women are entitled under the Equal Pay Act 1970 to equal pay with men when doing work that is the same, or broadly similar.

You have rights to equal opportunities. Exercise them.

The job of the Equal Opportunities Commission
The Equal Opportunities Commission has been created to ensure effective enforcement of the Sex Discrimination Act and the Equal Pay Act, and to promote equal opportunities between the sexes.

What is sex discrimination?
There are two kinds of discrimination.

Direct discrimination involves treating a woman less favourably than a man because she is a woman.

Indirect discrimination means that conditions are applied which favour one sex more than the other but which cannot be justified.

For example, if an employer, in recruiting clerks, insists on candidates being six feet tall, a case may be made out that he is unlawfully discriminating.

Your rights under the law
The Sex Discrimination Act 1975 and the Equal Pay Act 1970 both came into effect on 29 December 1975. They could have a considerable effect on your career prospects as well as your pay packet. Be sure that you understand your rights. Basically, they are as follows.

Employment
Employers may not discriminate against you because of your sex in their recruitment or treatment of you. This also applies to promotion and training.

Employers may not usually label jobs 'for men' or 'for women', but there are a limited number of exceptions. For example, in employment in a private household; in jobs where a person's sex is a 'genuine occupational qualification', as in acting; or where there are not more than five people on the staff. In employment it is also unlawful to discriminate because a person is married.

Education
Co-educational schools, colleges and universities may not discriminate in the provision of facilities or, from 1 September 1976, in their admissions. It would be unlawful, for example, to refuse a girl admission to a woodwork class because she is a girl. The Careers Service must not discriminate in the advice and assistance offered to girls and boys.

However, single-sex schools are permissible.

Housing, goods, facilities and services
With a few exceptions, no one providing housing, goods, facilities or services to the public may discriminate against you because of your sex.

Discrimination must not be used against you in the buying or renting of accommodation. A hotel, boarding-house or restaurant may not refuse you accommodation or refreshment.

A bank, building society or finance house must offer you credit, a mortgage or loan on the same terms that it would offer the facilities to someone of the opposite sex.

Advertising
Advertisements with job descriptions such as 'waiter', 'salesgirl', 'postman', or 'stewardess' will be deemed to discriminate, unless they contain an indication that both men and women are eligible.
(Only the Equal Opportunities Commission can bring proceedings in matters to do with advertising.)

Victimisation
It is important to remember that the law will also protect you if you are victimised for bringing a complaint.

Where you may bring your complaint
If you feel that you have been treated unfairly because of your sex, you have the right to take your complaint to a county court in England or Wales, or sheriff court in Scotland. If your grievance is to do with employment, you go to an industrial tribunal.

29 The Sex Discrimination Act

Ever since the First World War women have been fighting for equality with men. In 1928 they received equal voting rights and now women are increasingly found in leading positions in politics, industry and elsewhere. In recent years the Women's Liberation movement has insisted on even more equality. Their efforts possibly played a part in the passing of the legislation described on the opposite page.

Comprehension

1   *a*   How long has the Sex Discrimination Act now been in force?

     b   Does the Act protect men, women or both men and women?

     c   In fact is it men or women who have suffered most through sex discrimination?

     d   There is a statement near the beginning of the leaflet which summarises the purpose of the Act. What is it?

     e   Does the Act directly affect the husband and wife in a marriage? Does it mean that housework, care of the children and earning the salary must be equally divided?

     f   What did the Equal Pay Act of 1970 mean?

     g   Which body has the responsibility of making sure that the Sex Discrimination Act and the Equal Pay Act are successful?

     h   What is the difference between direct and indirect discrimination?

     i   Give three situations from the leaflet which are outside the Act.

     j   Can you think of an example of a job where a person's sex is a 'genuine occupational qualification', apart from acting?

     k   Does the Act mean that in future there can be no separate boys' schools and girls' schools?

     l   In the past women have sometimes been at a disadvantage in dealing with banks and borrowing money from building societies. Have they now the same rights as men in this respect?

     m   If you want to complain that something is against the Act, why should you not need to worry that you will suffer by complaining?

     n   If you think that you have not been given promotion in your job simply because of your sex, who should you go to?

Composition

1 (O)   You are an official of the Equal Opportunities Commission and you have been invited to give a talk about the Sex Discrimination Act to a group of young people who are about to leave school and start work or go to college or university. Make a list of points from the opposite page which you think will be important to them and give your talk.

2 (W)   Write to the Equal Opportunities Commission describing briefly a case of sex discrimination in which you have suffered and asking for advice on what you should do.

3 (W)   Using the main points in the leaflet and excluding the less important points, write a composition on 'The Sex Discrimination Act of 1975' in 120-180 words.

Immigration

Genuine students from abroad are welcome to enter Britain and to remain for the period of their studies, but the basis on which they are admitted is that they are expected to leave when their studies are completed.

If you are a *foreign national* (other than a national of a member state of the EEC) you may need to obtain a visa from the nearest British official representative before setting out on your journey, although many countries now have visa abolition agreements with Britain. You should make enquiries locally to find out if you need one. Foreign nationals who do not require visas are strongly recommended to apply to the nearest British official representative for a Home Office letter of consent. Possession of such a letter is not obligatory but should greatly facilitate entry, and in the unlikely event of being refused leave to enter, the holder would have the right of immediate appeal to an independent adjudicator. All foreign nationals (except EEC nationals) must obtain leave to enter from the immigration officer on arrival at a British port. He will expect you to produce evidence in the form of a letter from a university, college of education or further education, an independent school or any bona-fide private educational institution showing that you have enrolled for a full-time course of study and evidence of your ability to meet the cost of the course and maintain yourself and any dependants financially, without working, during your stay. Full-time study is regarded as involving at least 15 hours a week of organised day-time study of a single subject or of related subjects.

If you are a *national of a member state of the EEC* you may be admitted to Britain simply upon production of a valid passport or national identity card. You do not need to obtain a visa or a letter of consent nor would you normally be asked by the immigration officer to produce evidence of your enrolment for a course of study. Leave to enter is usually given for an initial period of six months and no employment restrictions are imposed.

If you are a *Commonwealth citizen* and you seek entry as a student, you will be required by the immigration officer at the port of arrival to produce evidence that you have enrolled for a course of study at a university, college of education or further education or an independent school or any bona-fide private educational institution. You will also be asked to show that adequate funds will be available to meet the cost of fees, your own maintenance and that of any dependants during your stay. Before setting out for Britain it is wise to apply, in good time before your departure, to the nearest British official representative for an entry certificate. Entry certificates are not obligatory for students, but an application for one makes it possible to clear up beforehand any doubts about your eligibility for admission to Britain. In support of your application you should be able to show proof that you have been accepted for a course of full-time study; this normally involves attendance for a minimum of 15 hours a week in the organised day-time study of a single subject or related subjects. An entry certificate is unlikely to be issued if you have *not* already enrolled for such a course. You may be required to produce evidence of your previous academic achievements, and the entry certificate officer will ask you about the subjects you are to take and the length of your proposed course. In addition he will need evidence that adequate financial arrangements to meet the cost of your course, your own maintenance and that of any dependants have been made on your behalf. A proposal to study only part-time, for instance at evening classes, will not justify the issue of an entry certificate.

If you are a *student nurse or pupil nurse* and are a foreign, EEC or Commonwealth national you will be classed as a student and most of what is said above will apply to you. You should bring with you to show to the immigration officer written evidence that you have been accepted for training by a hospital and it will be helpful also if you produce medical evidence of physical fitness including a chest X-ray.

If you are a girl over the age of 17 who wishes to come to Britain as an *au pair* in order to learn English you must have with you a letter from the family to which you will be going; this letter must state that the family have made firm arrangements to accept you as an *au pair*. You should also be aware of the principles governing the *au pair* arrangements. A leaflet in several European languages about *au pair* is available from the Home Office.

Immigration control

Before being allowed to enter Britain you will have to pass through immigration control where you will be asked for your passport and any health certificates that may be appropriate. The immigration officer will place in your passport an endorsement which will notify you of the length of time you may stay and of any additional restrictions imposed upon you. If you wish to stay longer than the time allowed (or to have any of the other conditions of entry varied or revoked), you can apply to do so by writing, at least two months before the end of the specified time, to the Under Secretary of State, Home Office, Immigration and Nationality Department, Lunar House, Wellesley Road, Croydon, CR9 2BY. You must explain the reasons for your request and support it by sending a letter from the school or college confirming that you are enrolled for further full-time study, along with proof that you can still maintain yourself. Since you must also send your passport the letter should be registered or sent recorded delivery. An EEC national must send in either his passport or his national identity card together with his landing document and two passport-size photographs.

One of the conditions imposed on the entry of a foreign student may be a requirement for him to register at once with the police. If you are required to do so it will be shown in your passport endorsement. Registration in London will be at the Aliens' Registration Office, 10 Lamb's Conduit Street, WC1N 3NX. Outside London you should ask at the nearest police station for the address of the office at which you should report. You will need to take with you your passport and three recent passport-size photographs. The fee for registration is £2.50.

If you encounter difficulty at immigration control you should ask to see a representative of the UK Immigrants Advisory Service (UKIAS) and if necessary get in touch with your educational institution. In cases of difficulty with the Home Office *after entry*, advice can be obtained from your college welfare officer, from UKIAS or from the Joint Council for the Welfare of Immigrants (JCWI).

Holidays abroad and re-entry visas

You may decide at some time to spend your college vacation outside Britain. If you are a *foreign* national and required a visa to enter Britain initially, you will need a re-entry visa to show to the Immigration Officer on your return to Britain from holiday. You should apply for the re-entry visa at least one month before your date of departure from Britain on holiday to the Passport Office, Clive House, Petty France, London, SW1H 9HD. Before doing so you should check that your *leave to enter* Britain still has sufficient validity to cover the period of your holiday and return. If such leave has less than two months remaining unexpired you must first renew it by applying to the Home Office, Immigration and Nationality Department, Lunar House, Wellesley Road, Croydon, CR9 2BY. After renewal you should then apply for the re-entry visa to the Passport Office. In addition all students returning to this country from a temporary absence abroad should obtain a letter from their college confirming that they are still registered as full-time students at the college and that they will be returning to the college at the end of their holiday to resume their full-time course. They should also have in their possession evidence, such as a bank statement, to show that sufficient funds are available for their support in Britain for a further period. It is also open to Commonwealth citizens to apply while on holiday abroad to the nearest official British representative for a United Kingdom entry certificate before returning to Britain. Any application for an entry certificate should be accompanied by evidence of studies and funds.

30 Entering Britain

Entering most countries as a tourist is usually fairly simple, but entering for a longer stay is more complicated. Britain is no exception. To enter Britain and stay here to study you have to observe certain procedures and be familiar with certain regulations. In practice the Immigration and Home Office officials and the police may interpret the regulations on the opposite page with reason and flexibility but it is important to know what these regulations are.

Comprehension

1   Taking your information from the opposite page, fill in the following table to tabulate the British immigration requirements. If a document is obligatory, write 'O'; if it is not absolutely necessary but advised, write 'R' for recommended; write 'D' if possession of the document is dependent on the person's country (this will be useful in the last two categories).

		Passport or National Identity Card	Visa	Home Office Letter of Consent	Entry Certificate	Evidence of Enrolment on Full-time course	Hospital Training Acceptance	Evidence of Sufficient Funds	Evidence of Physical Fitness	Letter from British Family
1	Foreign National requiring visa									
2	Foreign National not requiring visa									
3	E.E.C. National									
4	Commonwealth Citizen									
5	Student Nurse or Pupil Nurse									
6	*Au pair* girl									

2   In the formal language of this leaflet many 'official' words are used which would not normally be used in ordinary, spoken English. In each of the following phrases, taken from page 62, replace the word(s) in italics with a simpler, more common word or words.

e.g. they are *admitted*
    they are allowed in
e.g. their studies are *completed*
    their studies are finished
e.g. may need to *obtain* a visa
    may need to get a visa

a you should *make enquiries*   *b* who do not *require* visas   *c* is not *obligatory* but   *d* should *facilitate* entry   *e* refused *leave* to enter   *f* to *produce* evidence   *g* *bona fide* educational institution   *h* an *initial* period   *i* you *seek* entry   *j* you will be *required* by the officer to   *k* *adequate funds*   *l* who *wishes* to come   *m* this letter must *state*   *n* you should *be aware of*

3   *a* How do you know how long you are permitted to stay in Britain?
    b How can you ask permission to stay longer than the original period given to you?
    c If you have to send your passport by post, what precaution should you take?
    d If you have to register with the police, what should you take with you?
    e What should you do if you get into difficulties at immigration control?
    f If you get into difficulties with the Home Office once you are in Britain, what three people or bodies may be able to give you advice?

4   *a* Which people need a re-entry visa, and how can they get one?
    b If your present leave to enter Britain expires in the middle of your intended holiday abroad, what should you do before applying for a re-entry visa?
    c What two things should an overseas student returning to this country have besides a re-entry visa?

5   In each of the following phrases, taken from page 62, replace the formal, official word(s) in italics with a simpler, more common word or words.

e.g. certificates that may be *appropriate*
    certificates that may be necessary

a which will *notify* you   *b* any *additional* restrictions   *c* conditions of entry *varied* or *revoked*   *d* if you *encounter* difficulty   *e* to enter Britain *initially*   *f* has *sufficient* validity

Composition

1 (O/W) Taking the necessary information from page 62, tell, or write a letter to, a friend *from your own country* about what he or she should do before coming to study in Britain. Use simple, common words.

2 (O/W) Taking the necessary information from page 62, tell, or write a letter to, a friend *from your own country* about *a* what will happen when he enters Britain, *b* what he should do during his stay in Britain.

3 (O/W) If you are in Britain now, describe your experiences at *a* immigration control when you entered, *b* with the Home Office since you entered.

4 (W) Read the opposite page again and write a letter to the Home Office asking for an extension of your permitted stay in Britain.

5 (W) Read page 62 again and write a letter to the Passport Office asking for a Re-entry Visa.

6 (W) Write a conversation between a student entering Britain and an immigration officer. Write in dialogue form giving only the speakers ('Student', 'Immigration Officer') followed by their words.